D0594240

Voice of Indigenous Peoples

Native People Address the United Nations

Native People Address the United Nations

Hopi, Lakota, Haudenosaunee,
Native Hawaiian: United States
First Nations: Canada   **Inuit:** Canada and Greenland
Wayuu: Venezuela **Yanomami:** Brazil
Maya: Guatemala   **Kuna:** Panama
Ainu: Japan   **Sarawak:** Malasia   **Masai:** Tanzania
Aborigine: Australia   **Maori:** New Zealand
Saami: Western Europe **Nanaetz:** Eastern Europe

Voice of Indigenous Peoples

With the **UNITED NATIONS DRAFT DECLARATION OF INDIGENOUS PEOPLES RIGHTS**

Preface by **Rigoberta Menchú**   Foreword by **Boutros Boutros-Ghali**
Edited by **Alexander Ewen** for
The Native American Council of New York City
Introduction by **The Native American Council of New York City**
Epilogue by **Oren Lyons**

CLEAR LIGHT PUBLISHERS
Santa Fe, New Mexico

Clear Light Publishers
823 Don Diego
Santa Fe, New Mexico 87501

Library of Congress Cataloging-in-Publication Data
Voice of indigenous peoples : a plea to the world / [edited by] Alex Ewen. — 1st ed.
    p. cm.
    Includes bibliographical references and index.
    ISBN: 0-940666-31-6 (alk. paper) : $12.95
    1. Indigenous peoples. 2. Human rights. 3. Human ecology.
I. Ewen. Alex.
GN380. V. 65 1994
306' . 08 – dc 20   93 – 36081
                                                                          CIP

First Edition
10 9 8 7 6 5 4 3 2 1

Cover photograph of Hopi Elders at the United Nations by Marcia Keegan

♻ Printed on Recycled Paper

The Native American Council of New York City is the representative and policy-making body for the 27,000-member New York City Indian community. The current council members are: Rosemary Richmond (Mohawk), Executive Director of the American Indian Community House; Tonya Gonnella Frichner (Onondaga), President of the American Indian Law Alliance; Alexander Ewen (Purepecha), Director of the Solidarity Foundation; Ingrid Washinawatok-El Issa (Menominee), Co-Chair of the Indigenous Women's Network; with Mark Michaels as Deputy Director and Kent Lebsock (Lakota) as Secretary.

All of the royalties from sales of the book will be donated to The Native American Council of New York City for the purpose of furthering international work on behalf of native peoples.

DEDICATION

Pedro Bissonnette (Lakota) U.S.A.—Murdered by police, 1973

Anna Mae Aquash (Micmac) U.S.A.—Murdered, 1976

Efrain Cabrera Quintanilla (ANIS) El Salvadore —Murdered by the army, 1990

Thirty-four villagers from Chilcahuaycco (Quechua) Peru—Massacred by the army, 1990

Porfiro Suni Quispe (Quechua) Peru — Murdered by "the Shining Path," 1991

Luis Quinchavil Suárez (Mapuche) Chile —"Disappeared" by the army, 1981

Velario Tamir Macuxí (Macuxí) Brazil—Killed while in police custody, 1988

Florencio Cáceres (Xicaque) Honduras—Murdered by land speculators, 1991

Vincente Matute Cruz (FETRIXY) Honduras—Murdered, 1991

Lourenco Yekuana (Yanomami) Brazil—Murdered by gold miners, 1990

Luis Napoleón Torres (Ahuarco) Columbia—Murdered by the police, 1990

Helen Betty Osborn (Cree) Canada—Murdered by assailants who were never prosecuted, 1971

Julio Cabasango (Quechua) Ecuador—Murdered by a local landowner, 1990

Tomás Diego Garcia (Mixe) Mexico—Murdered by police, 1992

302 villagers of Nenton (Chuj Maya) Guatemala—Among the 30,000 believed massacred by the army, 1980–1984

The *Mayan Indians of Chiapas*—Killed by the Mexican army, 1994

The *Tens of thousands of Indians* killed in the defense of their lands and culture throughout this hemisphere

Phillip Deere, Mad Bear Anderson, Lee Lyons, Daniel Bomberry, Frank Fools Crow, Mina Lansa, David Monongye, Reuben Snake, Corbette Sun Down, Bill Wahpepah, Tom Yellow Tail, Rudy Martin

And all other indigenous people who, with vision and determination, have dedicated their lives to the quest for the freedom and sovereignty of their peoples and nations

CONTENTS

Foreword, Boutros Boutros-Ghali 9

Preface, Rigoberta Menchú 16

Introduction, The Native American Council of
New York City 19

Native Leaders Address
the United Nations

Oren Lyons 31

Marcial Arias Garcia 37

Venerable Bemal Bhikkhu 40

Yevdokia Gaer 44

Lars Johansen 49

Poka Laenui 52

William Means 57

Ovide Mercredi 64

Giichi Nomura 68

Lois O'Donoghue 72

Moringe L. Parkipuny 77

Noelí Pocaterra Uliani 82

Tamati Reedy 87

Donald Rojas 91

Irja Seurujarvi-Kari 95

Mary Simon 98

Anderson Muutang Urud 103

Davi Yanomami 108

Thomas Banyacya   112
Epilogue, Oren Lyons   119

Regional Communiqués:
The Struggle for Survival

Central and South America, José Barriero   127
North America, Ingrid Washinawatok-El Issa   131
The Pacific Rim, Glen Alcalay   139
Africa and Eurasia, Alexander Ewen   145

Appendices

A. Statement of Indigenous Nations, Peoples,
   and Organizations   155
B. United Nations Draft Declaration of
   Indigenous Peoples Rights   159

Photographic Credits   175
Information Sources   175

FOREWORD
Boutros Boutros-Ghali
Secretary General of the United Nations

Today, on Human Rights Day 1992, we launch 1993 as the International Year of the World's Indigenous People. The theme chosen by the General Assembly is "Indigenous people—a new partnership."

It is no coincidence that we are launching this International Year on Human Rights Day. Many of the 300 million indigenous people in the world face social and economic disadvantage in the societies in which they live. In the past, some of the world's worst violations of human rights have been perpetrated against indigenous people. Today, indigenous people are often among the poorest, worst housed, and least paid. They usually have less access to education and welfare than other members of society.

For centuries indigenous people have lived on the margins of national and international life. Some have continued to live according to their traditional ways and have not adopted the predominant language or religion of their country. Many have been outcasts in their own lands. Rarely have they been incorporated by the larger societies in which they lived. Often they have been denied citizenship by the authorities of their states.

Often the ancestral lands of indigenous people were "discovered" by colonial powers and then allocated to foreign settlers. In many countries the indigenous people were relegated to reserved territories or confined to inaccessible or inhospitable regions. Some governments viewed as subversive those who did not share the sedentary lifestyle or the culture of the majority. Nations of farmers tended to view nomads or hunting peoples with fear or contempt. Many indigenous people seemed doomed to extinction.

Today, a welcome change is taking place on national and international levels. Many indigenous people have formed their own organizations. They are active in seeking improvements in their situations. In the last decade indigenous people have come in increasing numbers to United Nations meetings—the Commission on Human Rights, the Working Group on Indigenous Populations, and other conferences dealing with human rights, development, and the environment.

There have also been important changes in many countries which have benefited indigenous people. More and more governments have recognized the multicultural character of their societies. They have restored land to indigenous communities and supported institution building and socioeconomic programs for indigenous people.

The year 1993 will help to focus the United Nations system on the special situation of indigenous people and on their needs. One aim of the International Year is to provide help to indigenous people and communities in areas such as health, education, development, and the environment. The emphasis must be on practical action, in the form of concrete projects benefiting indigenous people. An important element of these programs should be the participation of indigenous people in their planning, implementation, and evaluation.

The commitment of the United Nations system to the cause of indigenous people is long-standing. It goes back to a time before the creation of the United Nations itself. This International Year is being organized in partnership by the United Nations Center for Human Rights and the International Labor Organization (ILO).

Since its creation in 1919, ILO has defended the social and economic rights of groups whose customs, traditions, institutions, or language set them apart from other sections of national communities. In 1953, ILO published a study on indigenous people. In 1957, it adopted the first international legal instruments specifically created to protect the rights of peoples whose ways of life and existence were threatened by dominating cultures.

My own involvement and commitment to these issues goes back to that time. I was a member of the committee of experts on the ILO Convention in 1957, and its Rapporteur. A major turning point came in 1970, when the Subcommission on the Prevention of Discrimination and the Protection of Minorities recommended that a detailed study be made of discrimination against indigenous populations. The report provided information, definitions, and recommendations for action by the United Nations. The work of Martinez Cobo, the Special Rapporteur, helped galvanize the United Nations system into action. A new and nonpaternalistic ILO Convention was produced in 1989.

The United Nations Educational, Scientific, and Cultural Organization (UNESCO), as part of its contribution to the World Decade for Cultural Development, has encouraged cultural expression and activities by indigenous people.

For the past decade, the United Nations Working Group on Indigenous Populations, which is open to all indigenous people and their communities and organizations, has considered international standards and guidelines for the treatment of indigenous people. Over 600 people from all over the world attended the Working Group's last meeting, in Geneva in July.

Some indigenous people's organizations are asking how the United Nations should now proceed. What should the mechanisms be for ensuring that the United Nations system consults, and takes account of, indigenous people? This is a matter for further reflection and discussion.

I have set up the Voluntary Fund for the International Year of the World's Indigenous People to provide resources for practical assistance to indigenous people. I appeal to all governments, nongovernmental organizations, and other institutions and individuals to contribute. Without a full financial commitment from governments the International Year will not be the success we hoped for.

It is important that this year should see the situation of indigenous people brought into center stage as a subject for public awareness and debate. Members of the media, teachers, nongovernmental organizations, and other individuals and institutions will, I hope, help stimulate discussion and provide information. Cultural events are extremely important in this regard. But the really crucial role of the United Nations is to promote and protect the human rights of indigenous people.

The way indigenous people are treated by states and the international community will be a major test of the seriousness of our commitment to a genuinely universal human rights regime. If we are serious about development, political participation, and human rights, we must address the special situation of indigenous people.

Soon this assembly will be asked to consider a draft of the Declaration of Indigenous Peoples Rights (see Appendix B). The adoption of such a declaration can be another milestone in the long struggle by indigenous people for recognition of their rights.

Agreeing on the text of the declaration and reaching consensus on the treatment of indigenous people will not be easy or straightforward. The situation of indigenous people changes widely. Some communities wish to preserve their distinctive ancient culture apart from the mainstream; others seek the path of integration into modern society. Some members of indigenous communities may wish to leave them; others may wish to pursue traditional cultures without change.

Similarly, the policies adopted by states differ widely. The political and legislative history of the Indian and Inuit communities of Canada is different from that of the native peoples from Brazil. Practices and attitudes, as well as the legal framework, are quite different in the United States as compared, say, to Ecuador. Australia and India, Botswana and Norway, approach indigenous affairs differently.

The balancing of individual and community rights is not easy, particularly when one civilization commands hugely greater material resources than the other. Human rights are universal, but the promotion and protection of the human rights of indigenous people require a special sensitivity to particular situations.

One thing is clear: the human and community rights of indigenous people will flourish best in an atmosphere of respect and mutual tolerance. If the majority society understands the values and achievements of indigenous people, it will be far more prepared to uphold their human rights.

Education and public awareness are therefore important. We are making progress. It is now clearly understood that many indigenous people live in greater harmony with the natural environment than do the inhabitants of industrialized, consumer societies. And the medical and botanical knowledge of tribal peoples—especially of herbal medicines—has begun to be recognized as a source of valuable knowledge for modern medical science.

It will take time for the international community to achieve agreement on principles which protect the rights of indigenous people and yet take account of the different situations across the world. By dedicating 1993 to indigenous peoples and the idea of partnership, we mark yet another milestone. . . .

This meeting is addressed directly to the indigenous people, but it concerns all peoples of the world. For the situation of indigenous people prompts us to take a broader look at human rights today. Henceforth we realize that human rights cover not only individual rights but also collective rights, historical rights. We are discovering the "new human rights," which include, first and foremost, cultural rights. The twentieth century has almost succeeded in reducing the world to the level of what some have called a planetary village—a village, perhaps, provided that cultural diversity is preserved in that village. But we cannot be sure that the twentieth century will hand down to posterity a favorable assessment, at least on that score.

A few months before his death, French historian Georges Dumazil noted with bitterness that, on the eve of the year 2000, the number of languages and dialects spoken throughout the five continents was only half what it had been in 1900. The modern world will therefore prove to have been a great destroyer of languages, traditions, and cultures. The latter are being drowned by the flood of mass communications, the instruments of which all too often remain in the service of a handful of cultures. Today, cultures which do not have powerful media are threatened with extinction.

We must not stand idly by and watch that happen. Diversity is another name for the world. What would the world be like if there were no differences? What would the world be like if there were only one language? It is true that, as Paul Valéry said, civilizations are mortal. But just because civilizations are mortal, that does not mean that we must kill them.

Allowing native languages, cultures, and different traditions to perish through "nonassistance to endangered cultures" must henceforth be considered a basic violation of human rights. An inadmissible violation. We might even say that there can be no human rights unless cultural authenticity is preserved. We have seen how a culture that is marginalized eventually disappears, and we know that when a community is left out of the mainstream of international life, it is very difficult for its members to reserve even the most elementary human rights.

We can no longer allow a single act of ethnocide to take place. Let us promise to be more vigilant in this respect than we have been until now. Let us organize the watch and let us sound the alarm as soon as a civilization, a language, or culture is in danger.

This International Year is well chosen, for our fight to defend indigenous people has just been acknowledged in splendid fashion by the awarding of the Nobel Peace Prize to Rigoberta Menchú in recognition of her work for social justice and ethnocultural reconciliation. I extend my heartiest congratulation to the new Nobel Peace Prize winner, and I am very happy to announce that Ms. Menchú has agreed, at our request, to serve as goodwill ambassador for the International Year of the World's Indigenous People.

The International Year of the World's Indigenous People coincides with an important year for human rights. The World Conference on Human Rights is to be held in June in Vienna. The international community is seeking by both events to illustrate one and the same value: the wealth of all singularity. It is time, for technology possesses in itself a tremendous power to level out differences. If we are not careful, it will gradually reduce men and women to mere interchangeable unity. The world will thereby be reduced to a single culture, a single language. That is to say, it will be reduced to the lowest common denominator of our dead cultures; and, although we will speak with one voice, we will have nothing to say.

I was saying a moment ago that the situation of indigenous peoples was of concern to us. In respecting them, defending them, in helping them to take their place in the community of nations and in international life, it is perhaps the world itself that we are protecting, according to the view that we have of this very diverse world. And, ultimately, we will be protecting every culture, every people, every unique being—in the final analysis, each one of us is a unique being.

PREFACE
Rigoberta Menchú

As we sit on the threshold of the twenty-first century, the struggle by indigenous peoples to protect their cultural identity, their collective and individual rights, and their present and future aspirations is now more dynamic and popular than ever. No longer should these ideals be denied in order to perpetuate discrimination against indigenous people. For those of us who have resisted during the past five-hundred years for the defense of our rights—and who have struggled for our very survival—our future glows full of hope.

The General Assembly designated 1993 as the International Year of the World's Indigenous People. The victory that indigenous people have achieved with this International Year, and the progress which is represented by the development of the Declaration of Indigenous Peoples Rights, are the result of the devoted efforts of nongovernmental organizations, the successful work of the experienced members of the Working Group on Indigenous Populations, and those sympathetic nation-states that have brought this issue into the heart of this great organization.

Our people have had a year dedicated to our issues, a year to organize activities which, by virtue of using the most reasonable forms of pressure and action, will contribute to the elimination of racism, oppression, and exploitation.

The United Nations proposals for 1993 should be matched by the endeavor of nation-states, governmental organizations, and nongovernmental organizations to resolve the problems which confront indigenous people. In the spirit of cooperation, they should strive to increase the participation of indigenous peoples in the planning, execution, and evaluation of those projects and policies which affect indigenous cultures, and they should work to enlighten their consciences and encourage respect for our cultures.

However, it is necessary to note that the current proposals are limited and do not fully address the needs nor the urgency of the indigenous plight, which is so much greater than what the general proposals for the International Year have addressed. Principally, there exist countries with significant populations of indigenous peoples that are not giving proper attention to this important step that has been taken by the United Nations.

We have made 1993 a year of struggle for the rights which have been historically denied to us. The problems which afflict the countries of this continent and other regions of the world can never be resolved satisfactorily without the full participation of the indigenous peoples of those same countries.

The recognition of the ethnic and cultural diversity of this world is an essential element in the progress of humankind. It is urgent that the economic, social, political, and cultural rights of indigenous people become the point of departure for recognizing and respecting important values, such as the concept we possess of the world and our relationship with nature.

I believe that proof of the respect and the acceptance of the indigenous people by the international community would be the approval of the Declaration of Indigenous Peoples Rights by all member-states of the United Nations. But this will only have validity if it is approved without diminishing the emphasis on those rights which must be maintained in order to truly put an end to the systematic spoliation which Indian people have suffered since the middle of this now-ending millennium. In countries like my Guatemala, this integral declarative message is inherent in defining a new future.

I would like to say a few words about Guatemala. As you all well know, there exists an armed conflict which has continued for thirty years and which has involved in one way or another the whole of the Guatemalan society, and in a way very well known to the indigenous people. I would like to make a solemn call to the negotiators in Guatemala to resume discussions and subscribe to the global accords over human rights, which would be effective immediately and which would be monitored by the United Nations, as the first step in the effort towards a negotiated solution to the armed internal conflict.

The Guatemalan Indians are deeply interested in the search for a political solution to the Guatemalan crisis, and we believe that, with solutions based upon previous requests, including the recognition of our rights and identity, the foundation can be laid for constructing a civil society and real democracy. This would be a contribution to the stability and the development of Central American and a step towards world peace.

Finally, I would like to confirm, in my position as Nobel Prize winner of 1992, my promise to maintain as my highest priority the noble causes of humanity, so that life can flower in its diversity, and peace can thrive with justice for all.

INTRODUCTION
An Indigenous Worldview

Over the past two hundred years the majority of people on this planet has shifted from an agrarian to an industrial society, losing their contact with the earth. They have become either so engrossed in advancing their own well-being that for them the earth is simply a tool by which to enrich themselves, or they are so poor that they have been left with no choice but to exploit resources for survival and destroy the very lands that sustain them. Then there are those whose cultures have driven them from appreciating anything but the narrow ministry of ideologues, or trapped them into the meager confines of their television screens.

In spite of these powerful curbs to thinking about the earth, there has arisen a view among millions throughout the world that the environment, indeed the very sustainability of humankind, is threatened. This view arises from the dramatic worldwide destruction and pollution of the last remaining areas of wilderness, a destruction that has been rapidly accelerating over the last ten years. It is an onslaught so terrible, so irreversible, that it could not fail to awaken a call for restraint. As the environment of the planet we all share, the source of life which many indigenous people call Mother Earth, continues to deteriorate after centuries of abuse, a philosophy that incorporates all living and nonliving things in its vision is being sought. Increasingly, people of all colors, cultures, and nations have been turning to the world's indigenous people: those of us who have lived on the lands of our ancestors since the beginning of history. Long proud of our tradition as "caretakers of the earth," indigenous people are combining energies to raise awareness of the need for everyone to become active defenders of the remaining wildlife and wilderness—a part of the world that has now become totally dependent on human generosity and sensitivity for its continued survival.

There are other onslaughts, less obvious perhaps, or less

critical to nonindigenous people, but equally alarming. We are the caretakers of the earth; our philosophies, religions, and governments have been oriented towards that goal. Many native peoples of North America live under original laws given by the Creator, instructing us to care for the land upon which we live, the water that sustains us all, and our grandfather the sky. The earth is nurtured and revered with great respect, for it is understood that it is greater than we are and that we depend upon her for our very survival. Those lands that are still in our possession we strive to maintain in their pristine state. We ourselves, however, are an endangered species and may soon, like the rain forests, disappear. Along with the assault on our peoples, our governments are colonized, our lands occupied and stolen, our religious freedoms denied, and our treaties broken. Our multitude of cultures is shrinking. Each time an elder dies in North America it is like a rare book that is lost forever. When whole cultures are lost, so are different ways of thinking, distinct perspectives and philosophies that allow humans and nature to live in harmony. At the same time as the world is rapidly being deprived of its biological diversity and its ability to sustain itself, it is also being robbed of the tools of thought that may counter this self-destruction.

While we have observed this onslaught with great pain, and in many cases have suffered along with our wilderness, we have also observed the changing views of other peoples as they strive to understand what is happening around them. This change represents a great hope for the world.

The United Nations International Year of the World's Indigenous People comes at an auspicious time and provides an opportunity to present a worldview, a comprehensive alternative, to the current vision of consumption and destruction. Beneath the mighty powers that are now the world's nation-states, our ancient traditions continue. We continue to practice the age-old ceremonies and stoke the low fires of free expression and clear thought. Though seemingly outdated and insignificant, our traditions have persevered in keeping our lands and our cultures intact. They are also a challenge to current thought and values, and a reminder that there exists the means and the will to change the troubled destiny of humankind. For us this International Year represents a historic opportunity for indigenous people to forge greater ties amongst ourselves, working together in our communities around the world, and to forge with our nonindigenous brothers and sisters a new partnership. "A new partnership" is what the United Nations' resolution creating the International Year of the World's Indigenous People has called for. A new partnership is not only imperative for indigenous people as we strive to save our societies, our territories, and our cultures, it is essential if the world is to work together to stop the current cycle of destruction which threatens the giver of all life, our mother the earth.

The Native American Council of New York City was originally formed in 1990 in response to a call from the Traditional Circle of American Indian Elders and Youth to address the five-hundredth anniversary of Christopher Columbus's arrival on our shores, the shores of Turtle Island. In 1990, when the elders and leaders met on the sovereign territory of the Onondaga Nation, native people gathered there expressed their desire that 1992 be declared the Year of the World's Indigenous Peoples. However, the United Nations declared 1993, instead of 1992, the International Year due to pressure from Spain, Brazil, and the United States, among others. Wisely though, our elders and leaders understood that 1992 and 1993 would give indigenous people from around the globe the opportunity to put our issues before the world for two years instead of just one. This is proving to be true. The Native Council's purpose was, therefore, not only to address the issues surrounding the "celebration" of Columbus's journey and its resulting effects on native peoples. In keeping with our worldview, and the direction of our elders and leaders, it was also to pursue education and active projects that would positively benefit our world, our environment, and our peoples.

The objection of indigenous people to the United Nations' original title, the International Year *for* the World's Indigenous People, resulted in the change of the name to the International

Year *of* the World's Indigenous People. For indigenous people, the use of the term *for* continued the same paternalistic attitude that has characterized many of our relations with the nation-states. Although indigenous people also wanted to make it the International Year of the World's Indigenous Peoples, in order to indicate our status as nations from a variety of places with diverse cultures, the United Nations would not agree to this change due to the favorable implications the "s" would have for the sovereignty of indigenous nations. Therefore, 1993 became the International Year of the World's Indigenous People.

The Native American Council of New York City was approached by various indigenous leaders and organizations in the fall of 1992 about hosting meetings of indigenous people surrounding the approaching United Nations' official opening ceremonies for 1993. At that time, members of the Native Council expressed their belief that if meetings were to be hosted in New York City, they should be open to indigenous delegates from all over the world who were interested in sharing critical problems and issues. The indigenous people assembled would be given the opportunity, in addition to meeting amongst ourselves, of jointly addressing representatives of United Nations' organizations regarding the International Year of the World's Indigenous People.

For the Council, the gathering of leaders, elders, grassroots activists, and individual members of indigenous nations was viewed as a historic opportunity that should be maximized for the benefit of our future and survival. It was agreed that it was critical to provide a platform for indigenous voices on the eve of the International Year. This platform would be one in which our views, ideas, complaints, and issues could be discussed amongst ourselves, unencumbered by the influence of the United Nations or the nation-states. To preserve the indigenous nature of the meetings, it was further agreed that it was important that the meetings be hosted and sponsored by native peoples and that despite the welcome support from our non-indigenous brothers and sisters, the meetings would be open only to indigenous people. A statement by Ingrid Washinawatok-El Issa, a member of the Native American Council of New York City and co-chair of the Indigenous Women's Network, summarized the spirit behind the meetings: "The Council is honored to host these meetings of worldwide indigenous delegates. Indigenous events sponsored by and for indigenous people were a common historical occurrence, and it is time to continue our traditions in this contemporary context."

The Native American Council agreed to make all of the necessary arrangements, and our co-host, the Continental Coordinating Commission, accepted responsibility for the lion's share of the fund-raising.

On December 8, 9, and 12, in New York City, indigenous people met in a grand council sponsored by and for indigenous people. No agenda was set for the meetings in advance. A list of potential issues that came to the attention of the Native American Council during the planning stages of the event was distributed to the delegates for consideration. The form and content of the meetings were, however, left entirely to the indigenous delegates who were in attendance.

By the end of the first two days, more than 250 representatives of indigenous peoples had attended at least a portion of the event. The delegates came from diverse geographical regions, continents, and indigenous nations, including the aboriginal peoples of Australia, the Saami of Norway, the Mapuche from Chile, and the Nanaentz from Russia. North American nations were strongly represented by Haudenosaunee (Iroquois), Lakota (Sioux), Diné (Navajo), and Cree delegates.

One result of the three days of meetings was a "Statement of Indigenous Nations, Peoples, and Organizations." On December 8, the first day of meetings, the assembly agreed to convene a committee to draft a declaration for the delegates to present to the United Nations on December 11, the date set for the indigenous peoples' meeting with the United Nations agencies. On December 9 the delegates began to discuss the declaration drafted by the committee. In lively debate, various specific and general comments were gathered about the tone and individual points summarized in the draft declaration.

When it appeared that a document to be drafted by the numerous delegates still in attendance would take days to complete in a line by line, bilingual critique, a second committee was appointed. This committee was asked to take the draft document, as well as the several comments gathered during the debate, and prepare a second declaration. The committee worked through the night to prepare this document, which is included in this book as Appendix A. Its eight points for action attempt to summarize the spirit and intent of the delegates assembled in New York City, although it was never generally approved by the gathering of nations.

Despite the many regions of the world that we represent and the variety of cultures we command, indigenous people worldwide struggle in the same arena: for preservation of our land base, the environment, religious freedom, culture, and language. In many cases, for our people involved in the conflict, these issues are life threatening. More fortunate indigenous people simply watch their limited land base shrink while what remains continues to deteriorate in a polluted world. Regardless of the severity of the threat, the message expressed by many of the indigenous delegates reflected the inability of the dominant culture to hear our voices or understand our point of view. A Lakota elder, Tony Black Feather, illustrated the point in a typically humorous way, with a story to the assembled delegates on December 12:

> It seems there was a Lakota spiritual leader who was sent to Rome to meet with the Pope of the Catholic Church. After his long journey, the Lakota set his teepee up in front of the Vatican, placed himself and his pipe in front of the teepee, and waited for an audience with the leader of the Christian faith. For four days and nights he waited in the heat of the day and the cold of the night with no recognition from the Pontiff. Finally, on the fourth day, the Pope said to one of his people that he had better go down and give a blessing to the Indian who had his teepee right in front of the Vatican. The Pope went down to the teepee and

without saying a word made the sign of the cross over the Lakota holy man. The Pope, satisfied, went back into the Vatican.

The Lakota holy man immediately jumped to his feet, bundled his pipe, took down his teepee, and quickly began his long journey home. When he got back, the elders asked him what had happened. He relayed the events to them and told them that finally, on the fourth day, the Pontiff had come out to the teepee and, since he didn't speak Lakota, said to the Lakota holy man in sign language, "take down that teepee and get the hell out of here."

At this point, action is required by the indigenous people to demonstrate their points of view. Education of the dominant culture about our issues, hearings on our treaties in an international forum, and constant and accurate exposure of indigenous viewpoints to the media are ways to facilitate communications and positive action for the benefit of indigenous nations.

On December 10, 1992, which was designated as Human Rights Day, the official opening ceremonies for the International Year of the World's Indigenous People were held at the United Nations. The events began in the General Assembly with speeches by member nation-states on the "new partnership," the theme designated by Resolution A/47/L.33 offered by Canada and read into the record.

The afternoon session saw thirteen leaders from indigenous nations from all over the world addressing the General Assembly. For the first time in history, indigenous people brought their issues directly to this international body. The gallery of the General Assembly was filled with indigenous delegates. The addresses by indigenous people opened with the blessings of Arvol Looking Horse, the Keeper of the White Buffalo Calf Pipe for the Lakota Nation, and ended with a historic address by Thomas Banyacya of the Hopi Nation.

The most disappointing aspect of the ceremonies on the tenth was the paltry representation of nation-states that stayed in the General Assembly chambers to hear our leaders speak. Although certain large Western nations, such as Canada and the United States, made sure at least one person was in attendance from their sizeable delegations, the General Assembly was nearly empty during the speeches of the elders. There were almost no representatives from Western European and the former Soviet Bloc countries, and representatives of many of the developing countries of Africa, South America, and Asia also failed to attend. Many of the indigenous delegates commented upon the apparent lack of interest of the nation-states in the United Nations' International Year of the World's Indigenous People.

It will require the vigilance of all of the indigenous delegates who attended the events in New York City during the week of December 7 to achieve positive, active results from the International Year of the World's Indigenous People. If the spirit of the theme of a new partnership is to be achieved in a sense greater than for a poster slogan, it will require not only the attention of the leaders of the world's nation-states, but the efforts of people of the nation-states, who must insist that their leaders listen to ours.

For many indigenous leaders who have been working for years to bring the issues of aboriginal peoples to the attention of the international community, the year represents an important first step. Our leaders from the four directions know that our people are facing critical issues that will ultimately determine the survival of our cultures, our nations, and our people. For all people it is increasingly apparent that the most important issue of survival is of the planet itself.

Today, the people in the forefront of this struggle are indigenous; it is the rain forests of South America, the pine forests of Quebec, and the tundras from Canada to Russia where native peoples take the front line in protecting the earth. The wisdom and experience of our leaders and elders is recognized more and more, and the world's peoples have acknowledged the need to examine different perspectives if any of us are to survive. Yet the international forums for this exchange are limited. The ceremonies at the United Nations on December 10, 1992, were therefore important in delivering our message to the world.

Although the United Nations represents people from around the world, all forms of government and the many colors that comprise the family of humanity, it will not officially hear the voices of indigenous people. According to the rules which make no place for the colonized, the General Assembly had to be adjourned in order for our leaders to take the platform. Nonetheless, their words were given for all to hear.

It is our desire to bridge the gap, to communicate our worldview to all people of this planet. The Native American Council of New York City, as host for the visiting indigenous delegates from around the world gathered in New York in December, is proud to make the text of our leaders' speeches available in this new book, *Voice of Indigenous Peoples: Native People Address the United Nations.*

This book is being published so that their words are not lost, so that their wisdom can be shared, so that their vision is preserved.

> The Native American Council
> of New York City

Native Leaders
Address
The United Nations

OREN LYONS
Chief, Faithkeeper of the Onondaga Nation of the
Haudenosaunee (North America)

I have asked two people, Arvol Looking Horse of the Lakota Nation and Ola Cassadore, who represents the Apache Nation, to join with me in representing the indigenous peoples of North America. Arvol Looking Horse is a spiritual leader of his people, and I have asked him to open this great event with an acknowledgment to the Creator.

Greetings. It is a part of our tradition to start with a prayer. I would like you all to pray for world peace and harmony and the International Year of the World's Indigenous People, 1993.

So, if you would stand up so that we may join our minds together as one.

[Arvol Looking Horse delivered the blessing in the Lakota language.]

I called for world peace and harmony. May peace be with you. Thank you.

This has been a long road for all of us. I am Oren Lyons of the Haudenosaunee,* and I am speaking on behalf of the indigenous peoples of North America, of this great Turtle Island. Mr. President, distinguished delegates, distinguished chiefs, clan mothers, leaders, and members of the world's indigenous nations and people, I bring you greetings. We thank you, the General Assembly, for the recognition and for proclaiming 1993 to be the International Year of the World's Indigenous People with the theme of indigenous people and a new partnership. We thank Madame Erica-Irene Daes, chairman of the Working Group on Indigenous Populations, for her consistent, dedicated, and enthusiastic support for indigenous peoples, and at this time we recognize the inspiration and spiritual force of Augusto Williamson-Diaz for his vision of such a day as this. And we send our gratitude to those indigenous leaders and people who also had the vision of this day for our peoples, who put their blood, their sweat, and their tears into this moment. To those who are no longer here, our profound gratitude and appreciation. We salute our sister Rigoberta Menchú for the honor she has brought to our peoples, and for her dedicated and unselfish work on our behalf.

This proclamation brings hope, inspiration, and a renewed dedication to our quest for self-determination, justice, freedom, and peace in our homelands and our territories. Indeed, the quest is a renewal of what we enjoyed before the coming of our white brothers from across the sea. We lived contentedly

* Otherwise known as the Iroquois Confederacy or Six Nations. The members of the Confederacy are: the Onondaga, the Mohawk, the Seneca, the Cayuga, the Oneida, and the Tuscarora.

under the *Gayaneshakgowa*, the Great Law of Peace. We were instructed to create societies based upon the principles of peace, equity, justice, and the power of the "good mind."

Our societies are based upon great democratic principles of authority in the people and of equal responsibilities for the men and the women. This was a great way of life across this great Turtle Island; and freedom, with respect, was everywhere. Our leaders were instructed to be men with vision and to make every decision on behalf of the seventh generation to come, to have compassion and love for those generations yet unborn. We were instructed to give thanks for all that sustains us. Thus we created great ceremonies of thanksgiving for the life-giving forces of the natural world—with the understanding that as long as we carried out our ceremonies, life would continue.

We were told that the seed is the Law. Indeed, it is the Law of Life. It is the Law of Regeneration. Within the seed is the mysterious and spiritual force of life and creation. Our mothers nurture and guard that seed, and we respect and love them for that, just as we love Ëtënöha, Mother Earth, for the same spiritual work and mystery.

We were instructed to be generous and to share equally with our brothers and sisters, so that all may be content. We were instructed to respect and love our elders, to serve them in their declining years, to cherish one another. We were instructed to love our children—indeed to love all children.

We were told that there would come a time when parents would fail this obligation, and we could judge the decline of humanity by how we treat our children. We were told there would come a time when the world would be covered with smoke, and that it would take our elders and our children. It was difficult to comprehend at the time, but today we have but to walk outside to experience the truth of that statement.

We were told there would come a time when we could not find clean water to wash ourselves, to cook our food, to make our medicines, or to drink, and there would be disease and great suffering. Today, we can see this, and we peer into the future with great apprehension.

We were told there would come a time when tending our gardens we would pull up our plants and the vines would be empty. Our precious seed would begin to disappear. We were instructed that we would see a time when young men would stride angrily back and forth in front of their chiefs and leaders in defiance and confusion.

There are some specific issues that I must bring forward on behalf of our nations and peoples. In North America: the issue of nuclear and toxic waste dumps on our precious lands and the policy of finding a place for that waste among the poorest and most defenseless of peoples today. Our environment is degraded by these waste dumps, by overfishing, by overcutting of timber, and by toxic chemicals from mining processes throughout our lands.

Another issue is that of violations of treaties that we have with the United States and Canada: there are 371 ratified treaties and agreements between the Indian nations and the United States. The Ruby Valley treaty of the Western Shoshone is a prime example of what the violations of treaties bring: human rights violations, forced removals, disenfranchisement of traditional people with confiscations of their property and livestock.

The refusal to recognize and support the religious freedoms of our people and the decisions of the Supreme Court which incorporate this attitude into federal law translate into the violation of sacred sites. Mt. Graham in Apache country is now a projected site for an observatory, causing great stress to the Apache peoples who have depended upon the spiritual forces of this mountain for survival. Ironically, a partner in this project is the Vatican, and even further it is proposed to name this project after Columbus.

The appropriation of our intellectual property is continuous and devastating.

Land is the basic issue. Land has always been the issue with indigenous people. Original title is a problem to all of you. We must try to reach agreement on a more level playing field that allows at least a chance for survival. Our brother, Leonard Peltier, has been too long in prison, and 1993 should signal a different attitude. What better way is there to send such a signal than his release after sixteen years of incarceration, a jailing symbolic of the exercise of dominion over our people?

All of these troubles have come from across the sea. The catastrophes that we have suffered at the hands of our brothers from across the sea have been unremitting and inexcusable. They have crushed our peoples and our nations down through the centuries. You brought us disease and death and the idea of Christian dominion over "heathens," "pagans," "savages." Our lands were declared vacant by papal bulls. You created laws to justify the pillaging of our lands. We were systematically stripped of our resources, religions, and dignity. Indeed, we became resources of labor for gold mines and in cane fields. Life for us was unspeakably cruel. Our black and dark-skinned brothers and sisters were brought here from distant lands to share our misery, suffering, and death. Yet we survive. I stand before you as a manifestation of the spirit of our people and our will to survive. The wolf, our spiritual brother, stands beside us, and we are alike in the Western mind: hated, admired, and still a mystery to you. And still undefeated.

So then, what is the message I bring to you today? Is it our common future? It seems that we are living in a time of prophesies, a time of definitions and decisions. We are the generation with the responsibility and option to choose the path of life with a future for our children—or the path that defies the laws of regeneration. Even though you and I are in different boats—you in your boat and we in our canoe—we share the same river of life. What befalls me, befalls you. And downstream, downstream in this river of life, our children will pay for our selfishness, for our greed, and for our lack of vision.

Five hundred years ago, you came to our pristine lands of great forests, rolling plains, and crystal clear lakes, streams, and waters. Since then we have suffered in your quest for god, for glory, for gold. But we have survived. Can we survive another five hundred years of "sustainable development?" I don't think so. Not with the definition of sustainable used today—I don't think so. So reality and the natural law will prevail; the law of the seed and regeneration. We can still alter our course. It is not too late. We still have options. We need the courage to change our values for the regeneration of our families, the life that surrounds us. Given this opportunity, we can raise ourselves. We must join hands with the rest of creation and speak of common sense, responsibility, brotherhood, and peace. We must understand that the law is the seed, and only as true partners can we survive.

On behalf of the indigenous people of the great Turtle Island, I give you my appreciation and thanks. *Dayhnato*. Now, I am finished.

Oren Lyons is a chief of the Onondaga Confederacy and a spokesman for the Iroquois Confederacy. He is a professor of American Studies at the State University of New York, Buffalo, and is among the most distinguished native leaders in America, having been honored by the United States and the United Nations for his work on behalf of indigenous people. The Iroquois Confederacy has the distinction of having the world's oldest continuously functioning democratic government, though at present it is under attack by the United States and the state of New York, which are attempting to undermine the sovereignty of the Confederacy and reduce the influence of the Grand Council of Chiefs.

MARCIAL ARIAS GARCIA
Continental Coordinating Committee of
Indigenous Organizations and Nations
(Central and South America)

W e realize that all of you who are present here are already aware of our many, centuries-old problems. In this respect, we come here not to tire you with the hundreds of issues which our people face at present. We come as the bearers of a message, a message which springs with great hope from our communities, and from our endeavor to provide alternatives and to contribute to solving these problems. We do believe that the problems of our people should be accorded the same prominence as other problems being considered by this world body. Likewise, in regard to items of concern to indigenous peoples, the discussions should be facilitated by the indigenous peoples themselves. It seems we will never stop being "indoctrinated, colonized, and manipulated." What we want is to be the leaders in the solutions of our problems.

We want this because of our belief that by affording us the proper respect, the world community will by degrees find solutions to the critical and ancient problems which human society carries with it. As proof of this, representatives of indigenous peoples affected by war have participated directly in peace negotiations, although their efforts were never recognized. We believe that it is only fair for the international community to recognize these efforts, as in the cases of El Salvador and Nicaragua. They should greet with enthusiasm the proposal that Nobel Laureate Rigoberta Menchú participate in the peace talks in Guatemala, seeking the calm and order which will enable the great populations of our indigenous brothers in that country to flourish.

We therefore propose the specific establishment within the United Nations of an Office for Indigenous Affairs, so that indigenous peoples themselves may make a direct contribution to the major problems which mankind faces today. We also believe that, to be able to move forward along this road, the states of the region should ratify and implement Convention No. 169 of the International Labor Organization, a convention which recognizes some of our ancestral rights.* At the same time, we must respectfully request that the senior officers

---

* In 1989, the International Labor Organization adopted Convention No. 169, the Indigenous and Tribal Peoples' Convention. Along with the ILO Convention No. 107, adopted in 1957, it is one of the few international instruments to protect indigenous peoples. Convention 169 provides for indigenous and tribal groups to maintain their ways of life without forced assimilation, and protects them from discrimination, cultural and religious oppression, and mandates environmental and social impact statements for development to begin on their lands. Once ratified by a member country, an ILO convention is binding on that country. Not unexpectedly, few countries have ratified Convention No. 169.

and diplomats present here hold a special session for 1993 to analyze and make proposals regarding the rights of sovereignty and self-determination for indigenous peoples. These subjects are neither idyllic nor utopian.

I would like to see the United Nations provide legal assistance and the needed technical training for indigenous organizations and societies and internationally and nationally promote legislation and reforms which will contribute to the recognition of the rights of indigenous peoples. A study on intellectual property rights of indigenous people being carried out by the Commission on Human Rights of the United Nations should be given priority. They should promote and strengthen indigenous education, culture, art, religion, philosophy, history, and indigenous sciences; return historic and sacred objects to the indigenous societies to which they belong; and they should prove that theirs is a genuine call for a new relationship with indigenous peoples by contributing adequate financing, which would guarantee the implementation of the actions I have mentioned above. Moreover, member countries should provide significant donations to the Voluntary Fund for future projects to be implemented and assure the direct participation in the management of these projects by indigenous peoples and organizations.

Lastly, we wish to point out the following: We regret that after ten years of sacrifices by the indigenous delegates in the Working Group on Indigenous Populations, the Declaration of Indigenous Rights has not been approved. We believe that this is due in part to the interests that colonial governments have in ignoring the indigenous peoples. We therefore urge the United Nations to approve this declaration.

Marcial Arias Garcia is the director of Kunas Unidas por Nabguana, the national Kuna organization of Panama. The Kunas are well known for their autonomous existence and their striving towards self-sufficiency through innovative development, such as fish farming. Garcia is also a director of the Continental Coordinating Committee of Indigenous Organizations and Nations, a hemispheric indigenous organization that was formed as a response to the Quincentenary of Columbus's voyage.

Venerable Bemal Bhikkhu
Chakma of Bangladesh (Asia)

M r. President, sisters and brothers, please allow me to speak a few words in my own language. *Jou Band-hulak. Mui Bangiadeshar Parbatya Chattagramma Chakma. Jou.* Greetings dear friends, I am a Buddhist monk from the Chakma tribes of the Chittagong Hill Tracts of Bangladesh.

My mother tongue is really the only thing which has been left to me. I have already lost my land, my traditional way of life, my family, and my friends. Today, December 10, 1992, is finally a day which marks a resurrection of hope for millions of people designated as indigenous or tribal. Let me present the situation of these people as I see it.

Throughout Asia you will find indigenous and tribal people. Their lives are a daily nightmare, an ocean of suffering. These problems have the same roots—disrespect for human beings and their rights. There is no respect for our culture, religions, or traditions. The situation has become so intolerable that there is now increasing violence, provoking even more misery. And the problem is not the indigenous and tribal peoples of Asia; it is part of a drama which dishonors the human condition, and changes must be made. But I have not come to complain nor to seek out the guilty. I have come to propose four actions to lessen suffering and bring peace.

The first is the right to truth. It is only by having the true situations known that we will be able to transform them. I ask, for all of us, that the Working Group on Indigenous Populations be made a permanent part of the human rights bodies of the United Nations. The members of the Working Group should be able to travel freely, to see the reality in our areas, and to make their findings known to the world's media as well as to the United Nations. Currently, the truth of the situations is too often hidden. Our only force is truthful information. Our lives are menaced because our situations are often unknown. Thus, the Working Group should have offices in many countries so that indigenous and tribal people can contact them. We will then be able to live in harmony with all the world.

Secondly, nations must acknowledge our right to land. Precise territory must be set out for the indigenous and tribal people. We do not want to be a museum for anthropologists, but we wish to be able to choose our style and speed of development. Thus, the working groups should encourage each parliament in Asia to guarantee, through laws, our right to land. The Working Group should monitor to see that these laws are respected.

Nations must also acknowledge our right to life and justice. We must put an end to massacres and prevent armed conflicts. When there is killing or rape, the accused must be brought to justice. The Working Group should encourage a respect for law when it has been weakened, for the impunity of guilty parties is an insult to justice and dignity. In order to avoid armed conflicts, there should be training in active nonviolence as practiced by Mahatma Gandhi and Martin Luther King. Thus, we ask that the Working Group organize such training, drawing on such persons as the Venerable Thich Nhat Hanh, Sulak Sivaraska, Adolfo Perez Esquivel, and organizations such as the International Fellowship of Reconciliation.

Lastly, the rights of the child must be acknowledged. You have had the wisdom to recognize the rights of the child by an international convention in 1990. For indigenous people, our children are our only hope. I therefore ask that UNICEF help to implement the rights of the children of indigenous and tribal people, especially the right to education. Most of our children are currently deprived of these rights through the lack of schools, teachers, and equipment. I therefore ask UNESCO to mark 1993 by giving fellowships for higher education to indigenous and tribal youth. If their potential is proven, these young people will help the whole society develop. I also ask UNESCO to help preserve and enrich our culture and religions, our identity, languages, and way of life. We are all human beings: not superior, not inferior. We have many things to learn from other members of the human community. And we must realize that we are interdependent beings and what you do has an impact on us, and what we do has an impact on you. In our eyes, the most precious resource is the human person. We wish to see harmonious development of the human potential—physical, intellectual, psychological, and spiritual.

In most of our families, the parents cannot properly feed their children. Our children are already carrying a very heavy burden of financial debt to the richest countries. For me, this burden is an injustice against those children.

In conclusion, we, the indigenous and tribal people, must also recognize our past mistakes. Often we have not fully respected the rights of the women in our cultures. Through education, UNESCO must help to promote the rights of women in our societies. We must also learn to renounce violence. We share a planet with other societies, and we must learn to live together in harmony. We are different but not enemies. Brothers, we have common enemies to fight together: ignorance, fear, hatred, and violence. We can be mutually enriched by our differences. The path of reconciliation between our people must involve respect for justice. There is no way for peace; peace is the way. Thus, the United Nations must promote a new human culture, that of nonviolence based on the respect of the person, the truth, and the rule of law. Thank you very much for your effort to know us, to recognize us, to understand us, and to listen to us. This cry of distress for your help comes today, this tenth of December, as a cry of hope from my heart. *Sabbe Satta Sukhita Hontu.* May all beings be happy.

Bamal Bhikkhu is a Chakma of the Chittagong Hill Tracts in Bangladesh. In the late 1970s, the Bangladesh army swept through the Chittagong Hill Tracts, located in central Bangladesh, burning hundreds of Chakma and Jumma villages and killing or wounding over 25,000 people. The Venerable Bhikkhu is a Buddhist monk who has dedicated his life to international peace.

YEVDOKIA GAER
Secretary General, International League of
Indigenous Nations and Ethnic Groups
(Northern Asia)

The small peoples of Russia have a special place in the family of peoples living on our planet. There are thirty-four smaller peoples in the European and Asian parts of the Russian Federation alone, including the Koryaks, Ostiaks, Kirghiz, Gilyaks, Saami, Nivkhi, and Chukchis. Their total population in Russia according to census data is in excess of 440,000 people. More than 17 percent of the total population of smaller peoples of the Russian Federation are still living a nomadic lifestyle.

The natural growth of small peoples* in the last decade amounted to only 16 percent. The small population and low rates of their growth have placed many of the smaller peoples of Russia on the brink of biological disappearance. At the same time, areas inhabited by smaller peoples are rich in unique minerals and raw materials, fuel and energy, as well as biological resources. If a balanced use were made of these resources, not only could these smaller peoples live at the level of modern civilization, but the strength of Russia in general could be increased by their use. Resources of the territories inhabited by indigenous peoples play a special role in the formation of the National Hard Currency Fund. They account for more than 30 percent of all hard currency earnings. These areas supply the world market with copper, nickel, timber, cellulose, fertilizers, furs, and more. The development planning of the territories of the small peoples of Russia on the basis of a hierarchical social concept is the main cause of their impoverishment. The implementation of this structure was particularly ruinous for the smaller peoples because they were small in numbers, greatly dispersed, and underrepresented in the state legislative body and in the executive system.

To avoid continuing tragedy in the lives of the indigenous peoples, the Parliament of the Russian Federation in 1992, for the first time in the history of our state, considered the social and economic problems in the regions inhabited by smaller peoples. The Parliament unanimously adopted a decision creating a new concept for development of the smaller peoples, giving their will and their desires the highest priority. The Parliament's decision and the president's decree adopted in 1992 allow the indigenous peoples to revive their traditional economic activities, to be the masters of the lands that were in their possession before. However, through a very complicated situation, the implementation of the Parliament's decisions has become difficult and prolonged. Speeding up this process is

* "Small peoples" is the official term for indigenous or tribal peoples.

only possible through unified action by state structures and public organizations.

The establishment in Russia in 1992 of the International League of Smaller Peoples and Ethnic Groups is a timely and important step. Its necessity and usefulness were widely supported by indigenous peoples and many ministries and departments of the Russian Federation, as well as by the Secretary General of the United Nations during his September visit to Moscow. The charter of the League is based on the principles of sovereign equality of all its members, and requires the unanimity of smaller peoples and ethnic groups in the implementation of the obligations assumed by them. It mandates the settlement of emerging conflicts only by peaceful means, with communities rendering collective assistance to each other. These principles promote a climate of equality and friendly relations among indigenous peoples and ethnic groups. The charter retains the spirit of cooperation in addressing issues of economic, social, cultural, and humanitarian development and encourages respect for human rights.

Activities of the League will focus on promoting governmental decisions and public initiatives aimed at reviving the economic and spiritual potential of indigenous peoples and other ethnic groups within the Russian Federation and within other states. The League conducts its activities in accordance with the norms of international law and the legislation of the states on whose territory the smaller peoples live. It strictly observes the principles proclaimed in the United Nations Charter. The League is open for all associations of smaller peoples and indigenous peoples. Its official languages are English and Russian, and its working languages are those of the smaller peoples themselves, depending on the need to communicate and assimilate information. In order to realize the goals that have been established and the principles I've referred to, the League will pursue the following tasks: the consolidation of efforts made by public organizations, business circles, and individuals striving for the revival, preservation, and development of smaller peoples; creating a fund for smaller peoples; developing the rational use of their natural, cultural, and historic environments; activation of efforts aimed at economic, spiritual, and physical development of smaller peoples; the attraction of constant attention on the part of states and the world community to the protection of the legitimate rights, freedoms, and other interests of smaller peoples.

The main activities of the League are the following: a thorough study of the economic, political, cultural, and language problems under the present and often obscene conditions in the member countries of the world community; the creation of a special monitoring system for the collection, processing, storage, and distribution of information characterizing the entire range of smaller peoples' problems; participation in development, export, evaluation, and implementation of government and other programs and projects aimed at the improvement of living standards of the smaller peoples; support by all possible means of scientific research to contribute to the development of the productive sector; improvement of environmental conditions and food supply; assistance to the vocational training schools of native peoples that are oriented to the preservation of the identity, intellectual development, and acquisition of job skills; participation in peace-building activities related to ensuring guarantees for the protection of rights and freedoms of smaller peoples; systematically informing world public opinion of the situation in the areas where smaller peoples reside; and the organization of a forum on smaller peoples' problems with the purpose of the revival, preservation, and development of smaller peoples.

The year 1993, which has been proclaimed by the United Nations as the International Year of the World's Indigenous People, will undoubtedly give a strong impetus to the adoption, by the government and Parliament of the Russian Federation, of several legislative acts defining a specific term for equal status of smaller peoples. Indigenous peoples of Russia, like all indigenous peoples of the world, do not have any time to engage in endless and fruitless debates. The International Year of the World's Indigenous People was proclaimed not to temporarily soothe the conscience of the United Nations and the world governments. It should become the starting point for meaningful, important work and for solving major problems of indigenous peoples of the world. Only common efforts can lead us to the path of civilized development, and on this path, the League will do its utmost to ensure the revival and development of smaller peoples and to provide assistance to other peoples.

Yevdokia Gaer is the secretary general of the International League of Indigenous Nations and Ethnic Groups, an organization that is the representative body of indigenous people known as "small peoples" of the Russian Federation. Ms. Gaer is also a member of the Peoples Congress in Moscow.

LARS JOHANSEN
Premier, Greenland Homerule
Government (Arctic)

I am pleased to be able to speak to you not only as leader of the Greenland Home Rule Government, but also as a representative of the collective Inuit communities in Greenland, in Canada, the United States, and Russia: all the indigenous people of the Arctic Circle. Since 1980 we have worked closely together in the nongovernmental organizations to make sure that our views could be heard in the international society.

When I was born, my country Greenland was a colony. During my youth, the country's status was changed from a colony to a totally assimilated part of the mother country. As an adult, I have played an active part to establish Greenland as a home rule territory in free partnership with the other parts of the kingdom to which we belong.* My experience shows that it is possible to change the world also for indigenous peoples. We will be dissolving the nation-states to which we belong and can take our independent and rightful place on the world scene, a scene which in these years is changing and embracing ideas such as democracy, freedom, and international cooperation.

The greatest threat to this progress today is racism. Let me point this out from the very start; that the struggle for indigenous peoples' rights is at the same time a fight engaged against the fundamental evils of racism and prejudice. Even though we in the Arctic have largely been free of this, indigenous peoples are all too well acquainted with the concept of ethnic cleansing. Unfortunately, we know the destroying power hate and violence between two peoples within the same country can have. It is a prerequisite for the fulfillment of the slogan of this year, "A new partnership," that we all combat our own racism and that we learn to worship the human being the way it was created—and that we learn to understand the beauty in our differences.

The United Nations is, more than any other forum, the place where liberation from colonization was made possible for many peoples whom today are called the Third World. Through the United Nations' decolonization program, political freedom, justice, and equality have been established for those people the world over. Today, we also celebrate Human Rights Day through the United Nations' Universal Declaration of Human Rights. A number of principles and international conventions for the individual's right to an independent, just,

---

* In 1978, the Parliament of Denmark approved self-government for Greenland and granted it jurisdiction over education, health care, social welfare, and economic development, effective May 1, 1979. With home rule, Greenlandic place names are now official; therefore the official name for Greenland is now Kalaallit Nunaat.

and equal life regardless of race, religion, or other affiliation have been established. Now it is the time for those of the earth's people who have been lost between these two great conferences of international cooperation.

The time has come when this international system must focus itself on establishing equality for us in the so-called Fourth World. We want our rightful place in the new world order. We hope that the United Nations International Year will show the world this and focus on the resources—political, economic, and commercial—that can help us to ensure that we, as the only people who until now have been neglected, are received not just as a true partnership with the globe's other peoples. The key word is "self-determination." We indigenous people from Greenland, Canada, the United States, and Russia have emphasized this many times both individually and collectively. We know from experience that there is great creative energy gathered in self-determination, both for us and for our mother states. Today, more than ever before, we know that no acknowledgment can replace the desire of a people to maintain their independent identity—the desire of a people to be the masters of their own destiny. Therefore, let us together make sure that this United Nations International Year will reflect this understanding of creating the international and moral conditions that will make this a year of self-determination for indigenous people.

Lars Johansen is an Inuit who is the premier of Greenland. Known as the Greenland Homerule Government, the new Greenland government has functioned autonomously, though still legally a part of Denmark, since 1979. Most of the 60,000 Greenlanders are of mixed Scandanavian and Inuit heritage.

POKA LAENUI
President of the Pacific Asia Council of
Indigenous Peoples (Pacific Islands)

In the spirit of aloha, I bring greetings to you, birds of many feather, in my native language. I am Poka Laenui, citizen of the nation of Hawaii. My friend, colleague, and fellow executive member of the Pacific Asia Council of Indigenous Peoples, Luisa Benson, a Karen national of the liberated areas of Burma,* is joining me here at the podium on this

---

* Karen are the indigenous people of Burma and Thailand who live in the last great teak forests of the world. The 4 million Karen of Burma have waged a forty-year

special day. We welcome with enthusiasm the United Nations call for a new partnership with indigenous peoples of the world. For me this is a time of special observations: 1992 observed the five-hundredth anniversary of the encounters of two worlds; January 1993 marks the one-hundredth anniversary of the invasion of my independent nation, Hawaii, by the United States;* and today we mark the opening of the International Year of the World's Indigenous People. Observations and anniversaries give us all a common time to reflect on acts and patterns of conduct, and so they are indeed important as we strive for a better world.

But why must we await such special times? Isn't every moment of cruelty a crime and every act of humanity a celebration? Should we not contemplate each day and each act with equal sacredness? I hope we will not have to wait another one hundred or five hundred years to revisit fundamental questions of cruelty and humanity.

We take the call for a new partnership as a sincere and hopeful sign of according indigenous peoples a place in the common work for human progress. As a first task, let us reexamine the definition of progress and the mode of achieving it, for a partnership can never work if there are no common values or aspirations. We cannot merely adopt patterns of conduct used over the past five hundred years without question. The domination theme, which has ruled the present evolutionary period of human development, has witnessed the institutions of slavery, imperialism, colonization, and eco-

---

struggle against the dominant Burmese to gain independence for much of the southern region of the country, called by the Karen *Kaw Thoo Lei*. While the country's name was officially changed to Myanmar in 1989, supposedly to include the other non-Burmese people, the name "Myanmar" simply means "Burma" in the Burmese language, and its use has been rejected by most of the world.

* The last sovereign governing Hawaii, Queen Liliuokalani was deposed in 1893, with the help of United States' troops, by an American named Sanford B. Dole, who then set up an independent republic. The United States then annexed Hawaii in 1898. The indigenous people of Hawaii are currently referred to as "Native Hawaiians" or "Pacific Islanders."

nomic conglomerations which have demoted the quest for spiritual development to the lowest rung of consideration. In the quest to dominate we have seen man's rampant destruction of his immediate environment and his insatiable hunger for further destruction in lands far from his own shores. None of those activities have raised the measure of happiness for human society one iota. Indeed, peace, joy, and contentment— requisites for spiritual development—can be experienced in the sight of waters running freely, in the sight of a man and a woman working side by side in their fields. I submit that in our new partnership, we explore not new ways of sharing in the domination process, but in totally new modes of conduct built on the respect of all things' right to be.

A second area for consideration as we build this foundation for a new partnership is the present systems' elevation of property and economic values above those of human values. Today, the primary model of a healthy society is one measured by economic standards such as the gross national product, gross domestic product, income flow, capital accumulation, and so on. Limited social resources are subsequently spent to improve short-term economic conditions. Development programs thus fail to take a holistic social approach, nor do they incorporate the values of strong cultures and healthy people, such as respect for the elderly and protection for the children; a pristine environment; an ethic of human rights and compassion within a society. Are not these values just as important, if not more important, in the measure of the health of a society?

We are looking for a shift in value priorities as we take a position of partnership with others. Developing principles and goals upon which we can act together as partners is one thing. But acting consistently within them is, clearly, another. For example, we have the highest regard for the Universal Declaration of Human Rights and all of the lofty documents and speeches on the subject. But we cannot accept a partnership of hypocrisy. How does an international body evoke such high principles and yet include in its membership countries which consistently commit gross violations of human rights? I speak of atrocities occurring in East Timor, West Papua, and the Moluccas Islands; in the Chittagong Hill Tracts, and in the territories of the ethnic nationalities of Burma.* We find insufficient action to protect the rights of people in these indigenous territories. Instead, many other members of the United Nations act in partnership with those violating elements by continuing to trade with, and to provide military training and support, to those very elements which are carrying out atrocities. We call for an end to such hypocrisy and for firm action to be taken by this institution to end such atrocities.

We are anxious to participate in many areas of work with the United Nations, and we ask that necessary steps be taken to permit us the needed entry into your chambers. Many of our people must obtain travel documents from those governments whose conduct we wish to have examined. Those governments in which United Nations offices are located must make special arrangements to permit any indigenous person, certified by international indigenous organizations, entry into their countries for the purpose of such work. Furthermore, indigenous representatives should have permanent places within the General Assembly to raise the special concerns of indigenous peoples from various regions of the world. If the United Nations is serious about a new arrangement with indigenous peoples, then structural changes must take place to bring about such an arrangement.

In closing, I should caution about the newfound enthusiasm with indigenous peoples, our cultures, our rights, our environmental attitudes and practices. Let us not be carried off into a

---

* The Chittagong Hill Tracts are located in Bangladesh. East Timor was invaded by neighboring Indonesia in 1975, which in the next five years proceeded to kill over 200,000 Maubere and other indigenous and nonindigenous Timorese, and has systematically reduced the rest of the population to abject poverty and fear. Indonesian rule over the Moluccas and West Papua, New Guinea (seized in 1963), has been no less brutal. From 1977 through 1979, the Bangladesh army swept through the Chittagong Hill Tracts, burning hundreds of villages and killing or wounding over 25,000 tribal people. Both these governments continue to be cruel oppressors of their indigenous peoples.

belief that indigenous peoples have the answers to all of the environmental, cultural, and relational challenges of the world. Indeed, we have every right to be proud of our cultural, philosophical, and historical roots, and we form an important part of the heritage of humanity. Just as other people have had the opportunity to proudly hold up their cultures, indigenous peoples should do likewise. But who among us have achieved the qualities of universal perfection? We indigenous and non-indigenous peoples are in a constant search for spiritual development, a search which has not ended. We must all share in that continuing quest as partners. We look forward to that challenge. Love the land, and aloha to all of you until we meet again.

Poka Laenui is a Native Hawaiian and the president of the Pacific Asia Council of Indigenous Peoples, an organization that represents the indigenous people of the Pacific islands and Southeast Asia. While ruled by an indigenous leader under a traditional government when annexed by America less than one hundred years ago, Native Hawaiians are not recognized by the United States as a sovereign people. Unlike Native Americans inside the continental boundaries, Native Hawaiians do not have reservations, do not have a title to land, nor do they have any special protections of their culture.

WILLIAM MEANS
President, International Indian Treaty Council
(North America)

I want to give you a traditional greeting in one of the classic languages of the Western Hemisphere, known as Lakota. *Hau. Mitakuipi ampetu kile chante ma wasté napa chuzau*. The translation means, "Greetings my relatives. Today is a good day, my heart is strong, and I extend my hand in friendship."

This has been a long road. I thank those teachers who had the wisdom to foresee this day. My teachers are Matthew King, Philip Deer, Chief Fools Crow, Kills Enemy, and Crow Dog. I come from the Oglala band of the Lakota Nation, also known as the Sioux. We are the people of the Black Hills and the upper Great Plains of what is now the United States. The Lakota Nation's legal relationship with the United States is governed by the bilateral international treaty signed on April 29, 1868,* which is similar to the other 370 existing bilateral treaties between the United States and the Indian nations within its borders.

I believe this empty room is somewhat significant in view of our long journey to this place. On behalf of the Indian people of the Western Hemisphere, the Red Man, and the International Indian Treaty Council, we welcome this new partnership between the United Nations and indigenous people. Today, we are especially proud of a member of our board of directors, Rigoberta Menchú, as she receives the Nobel Peace Prize in Oslo, Norway.

It is indeed an honor to address the General Assembly when, for the first time in history, Indian people of the Americas and indigenous peoples throughout the world stand before our peer member-nations of this great body to extend our philosophical worldview and our own contributions to the development of world civilization. As our leaders have often stated: There is only one voice, there is only one color of mankind, that is absent from this community of nations—that is the Red Man of the Western Hemisphere. This has been a long journey to get here today.

The longest war in world history has been the war against indigenous peoples. Until this moment, we have had our place in civilization determined by the so-called "modern," industrial nations, and were ranked according to their values—which have placed indigenous people at the very bottom of the human family. Today, the United Nations begins the process of knowing us, not through the distorted history of the colonizer, but by hearing our own voices, looking into our hearts, and understanding our humanity—to really begin learning

* The 1868 Treaty of Fort Laramie. A bilateral treaty is one between equals, therefore nation-to-nation.

about the important past of indigenous people and our potential contributions to the world. Today, we begin the process of seeing indigenous peoples of the world, not as primitive and backward, but rather as human beings with our own dreams and aspirations, our own value systems, and our own yearning for international recognition of our human rights, including the right to self-determination.

Just as the international community has recognized the right of self-determination for peoples in former colonies, the right of self-determination for indigenous peoples should now be recognized by the same international community. In the case of indigenous peoples of North America, this self-determination is already addressed through existing bilateral treaties. For years, indigenous peoples have been the mysterious minority populations scattered throughout the nations of the world, forgotten while the nation-states around them have been racked by violence and bloodshed. That is, forgotten until their natural resources are needed—which in turn means the loss of additional land for indigenous peoples. We are the Palestinians of the Western Hemisphere.

Might does not make right. Sovereign people of varying cultures have the absolute right to live in harmony with Mother Earth so long as they do not infringe upon the sacred rights of other peoples. The denial of this right to any sovereign people, such as the indigenous nations you see present, must be challenged. World concern must focus on all colonial governments so that sovereign people everywhere shall live in peace, with dignity and freedom. Former indigenous nations and tribes now strain against the artificial and temporary adhesive of colonial empires. Despite intense efforts at acculturation and assimilation by the great multinational forces and empires, the indigenous people of the world still cling to their own cultures, origins, and their indigenous roots. This has created a new tension in the world, where those who still maintain an attachment to those old multinational empires desperately try to hold together that which appears doomed to come apart.

The issue for indigenous peoples is the land. Indigenous people are one with the land. Many people, despite having indigenous blood flowing through the veins of their populations, move to eradicate their own links to their indigenous past by the eradication of any remaining living symbols of these links. Certainly, these actions continue to pose a threat to the very physical and cultural existence of the indigenous peoples of the world. The International Year of the World's Indigenous People is even more vital at this time because of this continuing and very real threat. This year sends a powerful message to those attempting to erase indigenous identity in their own nations—that yes, indigenous peoples do have human rights and deserve the greatest protection. Indigenous people have more than just minority status within the geographical boundaries of the lands wherein they live.

We know and understand our mother the earth and are humble in her presence because we know, and have known for thousands and thousands of years that we exist only with her sustenance. We know and understand humans and other living things on this earth, and we know that all living things are related; that all of life is woven together. Injury to one part of the world causes injury to the whole. This is our worldview— the sacred map that guides us throughout our lives—and one of the many contributions we are willing to share with the world, with the international community, and especially here at the United Nations if given a chance as a part of this new partnership.

The religion of the Red Man has never been institutionalized. We have never had missionaries, and we never tried to make an eagle out of a crow. One of our great Indian leaders once said: "Our land is more valuable than your money. It will last forever. Your money will perish by the flames of fire. As long as the sun shines and the water flows, this land will be here to give life to men and animals. We cannot sell the lives of men and animals, therefore we cannot sell our land. It was put here for us by the Great Spirit, and we cannot sell it because it does not belong to us. You can count your money and burn it. But only the Great Spirit, the Creator, can count the grains of sand and the blades of grass of these plains. As a present to you, we will give you anything we have that you can take with you. But the land, never!"*

As the attention of the United Nations is focused in the coming year on the situation of indigenous peoples of the world, we ask and encourage the General Assembly to consider one or more pan-indigenous and pan-Indian organizations to be granted Observer status within the General Assembly. I see you have some vacancies—because of the turn of events in the world—and we will gladly fill those. We ask that you include indigenous peoples in the enforcement of existing standards such as the Treaty on Genocide and the Universal Declaration of Human Rights. Both are beautiful documents that have closed the door to indigenous peoples. We are further requesting that members of the United Nations support a process that will lead to an International Convention for the Protection of the Rights of Indigenous People. We call for this international process leading to international legal mechanisms because indigenous people are in particularly vulnerable positions that existing legal norms seem unable to protect. Furthermore, such legal mechanisms would send a message to some existing governments with records of human rights abuses against indigenous peoples. Such legal mechanisms and expressions of international concern are critical to the survival of indigenous peoples.

Today is a new day. As the world changes, the United Nations must change also. A new spirit within the United Nations of international cooperation and action to secure human rights of ethnic populations, such as those in Eastern Europe, is indeed promising if such principles of cooperation

* Attributed to a Blackfoot chief in 1855.

and action are applied evenly throughout the world. We are hopeful that the same international cooperation and action will be forthcoming to protect the indigenous peoples of the world. We ask the General Assembly to recognize indigenous people and issue a report on the International Year of the World's Indigenous People at the opening of the General Assembly in September of 1994. We support the establishment of a Center for Indigenous Studies as a permanent agency within the United Nations. In the Americas there are over 80 million Indian people. In at least six countries in Central and South America the overwhelming majority are Indian people. As democracy spreads around the world, it is inevitable that in the near future an Indian nation will finally take its rightful place here in the family of nations.

We do not ask the United Nations to solve our problems. Indian people will solve Indian problems. We ask the United Nations for a partnership so that we can begin to study those international instruments that already exist and their application to indigenous peoples. Human rights violations continue from north to south, from Alaska to Tierra del Fuego. The rain forest of the Amazon basin, the lungs of Mother Earth, continues to be ravaged by industrialization, endangering the lives of the entire human family. Treaty violations continue throughout North America, especially in the area of the exploitation of natural resources. Racism is a major problem in the Americas. As Indian people still living on the land of our ancient ancestors, we have the absolute right to self-government, sovereignty, and independence. The industrial world must understand that our land, our Mother Earth, is not for sale; that the graves of our ancestors must not be desecrated; and that we are all related.

In conclusion, I would like to quote from one of our great chiefs, who was speaking to a military commander as his people were being rounded up to be put in concentration camps. His words, spoken in the last century, are most appropriate today. Chief Seattle, of the Suquamish Nation,* had this to say: "You Europeans did not weave the web of life, you are only a single strand in it. Whatever you do to the web, you do to yourself. Tribe follows tribe, nation follows nation. It is like the waves of the sea, it is the order of nature and regret is useless. Your time of decay may be distant, but it will surely come. For even your god who walks and talks to you as friend to a friend cannot escape the common destiny. We may be brothers and sisters after all. We shall see." *Mitakuye Oyasin.* To all my relations.

William Means is a Lakota from South Dakota and the president of the International Indian Treaty Council, a United States-based organization that works internationally for the rights of indigenous peoples. William Means was an early member of the American Indian Movement, a popular political group that helped transform Indian politics in the United States during the 1970s. He was recently the principal of the Little Red School House in Minneapolis, Minnesota, a school nationally known for its language and cultural education of native children.

* While known today as Seattle, he was Chief Sealth of the Duwamish. In the speech, given at the forced signing of the Treaty of Point Elliot in 1855, he is also representing the Suquamish Nation.

OVIDE MERCREDI
Grand Chief of the Assembly of First Nations
(North America)

On behalf of the Assembly of First Nations* from Canada, I would like to express, first, our gratitude to the members of the United Nations for providing us with this opportunity to speak about the importance of the International Year of the World's Indigenous People that we are

---

* "First Nation" is the official Canadian term for Indian nations, and "aboriginal" is the term for indigenous. First Nations do not include the Inuit (Eskimos), who are indigenous peoples yet are distinct from Indians.

inaugurating on this Human Rights Day. Where I come from, we have fifty-three distinct First Nations, each with the right and capacity to represent themselves. Unfortunately, we cannot represent ourselves in the way we would like to and unfortunately, from time to time, we have to comply with the rules as we did in this case.

I believe that it is very important to end colonization as it affects all of humanity, because decolonization is a right for all human beings, including the indigenous people around the world. We have experienced great pain, great turmoil, and we have lost land, resources, and lives in the experience that we all share in common as colonized peoples. Where I come from, the Beothuk Nation* became a victim of genocide in my country, just as around the world we know of other examples of other nations, indigenous nations, that have become victims of genocide.

We as a people denounce violence. We condemn governments that participate in acts of genocide against our indigenous brothers and sisters, and as an organization we have become awake and alive to the perils of our brothers and sisters in other parts of the world. We have become active and determined to isolate governments, such as the governments of Peru, Columbia, and Guatemala, for engaging in acts of genocide against their defenseless people. We are very proud today of the fact that our sister, Rigoberta Menchú, an indigenous woman of Guatemala, has received on this Human Rights Day in Oslo, the Nobel Peace Prize for the struggle to liberate her people from acts of violence. We applaud her courage. We support her vision for a nonviolent society in her country.

This morning we heard the Canadian government representative to this assembly, who spoke of the need for a new partnership and the importance of creating new relationships based on respect for each other. Sometimes the truth must be told, and on this day I regret to say that we were not consulted nor involved

---

* Shanawdithit, the last of the Beothuk Indians who lived in Newfoundland, died in 1829.

by our country in developing this statement that was read by the government of Canada.

We know from reading the history of our people and observing the history of other indigenous people around the world that we are not alone in experiencing the destruction of our culture, our language, and our way of life. We entered, with the nation-state called Canada, into a number of treaties on a nation-to-nation basis, believing that these treaties would be a basis for future relations; that they would be a basis for maintaining this coexistence that is essential amongst the peoples of this planet. The unfortunate truth is that in the country where I come from the treaties have yet to be fully implemented and honored by the Canadian government. These treaties were entered into by the people I represent with the best of intentions and goodwill, as a way of sharing land and resources, as a way of ensuring the integrity of their own society and the economic security of their own people.

Although in more recent times we perceive more receptiveness by the Canadian people and their government to understand our particular vision as indigenous people, we challenge the Canadian government to meet the needs of our people in the year 1993. We challenge them not to get involved in meaningless objectives—like the poster competition—as a way of drawing attention to the International Year of the World's Indigenous People. We call upon the Canadian government for direct action with respect to the rights of our people. We call upon them to honor and implement the treaty rights of the First Nations in Canada. We call upon the Canadian government to ensure that we have the land, water, and resources to sustain our economy and to guarantee our development as distinct people. We call upon the Canadian government to recognize the inherent right of self-determination of the indigenous people in Canada. We ask them to give hope to our people—not just words, but meaningful hope—by implementing the inherent right of our people to self-government by removing impediments and not creating new ones. We also call upon the Canadian government to deal with the real needs of the people we represent. We call upon them to address the poverty, not by attacking the deficit in our country, but by attacking the poverty of the poor people in our country, of whom by far the majority are the First Nations of our country.

There are many things that can be done at the United Nations level. Some ideas and recommendations made to you by Erica Daes we endorse. But as a first step and as a concrete sign of goodwill, we ask all the members of this assembly to support a resolution creating, within this agency, a commission on indigenous peoples under the auspices of the Secretary General of the United Nations, whose mandate would include monitoring human rights violations and ensuring the development of indigenous peoples around the world. As peoples and nations we also respectfully demand that the United Nations begin to look at reforms within its own structure of government to ensure that we have direct participation in the decision-making processes that were referred to earlier by other speakers. We call upon the governments of the world to begin to meet with us as equals, to respect our people as human beings, and to embrace our collective rights; to end this history of dominance and to replace it with what needs to be done to create a new era, a new world, where all people can live in harmony.

In concluding my comments, I just want to say that whatever I have said was not intended in the spirit of unkindness. What needed to be said, had to be said. But we look forward to a new relationship with the Canadian people and their governments, and likewise to a new relationship with other governments and other peoples in the world. We need to respect each other, we need to embrace our collective rights, and we need to eliminate this history of dominance that we have experienced for the past five hundred years.

Ovide Mercredi is a Cree chief who is also the Grand Chief of the Assembly of First Nations, the national native organization in Canada. Due in part to the fragmented state of Canada itself, the Assembly has been very influential in mainstream Canadian politics, more so than any equivalent organization in the United States. Because of continuing conflict between natives and the Canadian government over contested land titles and unsettled land claims, Canada has become a hotbed of indigenous unrest.

GIICHI NOMURA
Executive Director, Ainu Association of Hokkaido
(Northeast Asia)

Today, December 10, is Human Rights Day, marking forty-five years since the adoption of the Universal Declaration of Human Rights, a day which should rightly be commemorated by all mankind. Moreover, I can safely say that as the occasion of the inauguration of the International Year of the World's Indigenous People, today is a day that will remain deeply engraved on the memory of indigenous peoples. For the Ainu, who have formed a distinct society and culture in Hokkaido, the Kuril Islands, and southern Sakhalin from time immemorial, there is yet another reason why today will have a special significance in our history. This is because up until 1986, a mere six years ago, the government of Japan denied even our very existence in its proud claim that Japan, alone in the world, is a "mono-ethnic nation." However, here today our existence is being clearly recognized by the United Nations itself. Had these ceremonies been held a few years earlier, I would probably not have been able to make this speech as the representative of the Ainu people. In the eyes of the government, we were a people whose existence was not to be admitted. However, you need not worry. I am most definitely not a ghost. I am standing here firmly before you.

In the latter half of the nineteenth century, the land of the Ainu people was unilaterally appropriated by the government of Japan under the auspices of a large-scale colonization and development project known as "Hokkaido Kaitaku." We were forced to become a part of the Japanese nation. As a result of border negotiations between the Russian and Japanese governments, our traditional territory was carved up, and many of our people suffered forced relocations. Moreover, the Japanese government pursued an aggressive policy of assimilation from the very beginning. Under this doctrine of assimilation, the Ainu language was banned, our traditional culture was denied, our economic livelihood was destroyed, and the Ainu people became the object of oppression, exploitation, and severe discrimination. We were unable to continue our traditional way of life in our ancestral lands, as fishing became "poaching" and cutting wood in the hills was branded as "theft." This is an experience common to indigenous peoples everywhere.

Although Japan was reborn as a democratic nation after the Second World War, the policy of assimilation has continued while severe discrimination and economic deprivation remain. Unfortunately, this situation is not even seen as worthy of serious government investigation in Japan, which has never taken our rights as an indigenous people into consideration, although we have been petitioning the government since 1988 for legislation that would provide some minimum guarantees of our rights and dignity as a people.

However, I did not come here to dwell upon the past. In the spirit of the International Year of the World's Indigenous People, the Ainu call upon the governments of Japan and the member-states to enter into "a new partnership" with indigenous peoples. We call for the removal of injustices through cooperation and negotiation—values that were at the heart of our traditional societies. We invite the government of Japan to enter into a dialogue with us, as partners in an effort to create a viable role for indigenous people in the future of Japan. This is not merely a domestic issue; the overseas activities of Japanese corporations and the foreign aid efforts of the Japanese government are having serious effects on the world. This situation is linked to the indifference shown towards indigenous people within Japan. Through a new partnership, we believe the government of Japan will come to realize its responsibilities, not just towards the Ainu but towards all indigenous peoples.

In more concrete terms, as an indigenous person living within a highly assimilationist and industrialized society such as Japan, the Ainu request that the United Nations move rapidly to set international standards that guarantee the rights of indigenous peoples against various forms of ethnocide. Furthermore, as an indigenous person from Asia, where there has never been a tradition of considering the rights of indigenous peoples, the Ainu urgently request that the United Nations set up an international agency to clarify the situation of indigenous peoples, and put in place a mechanism for positive financial support of this agency by member-states.

The Ainu people, through negotiation with the Japanese government, desire the implementation of the rights of indigenous peoples being presently discussed here at the United Nations, including the right to self-determination as a people. How- ever, we do not perceive this right to self-determination as a threat to the national unity and territorial integrity of member-states. What we are after is a high level of autonomy based on our fundamental values of "coexistence with nature" and "peace through negotiation." We do not seek to create new states with which to confront those already in existence. We aim to achieve, through our traditional values, the development and realization of a society in which all peoples can live together in dignity. In the Ainu language, we have a word, *Ureshi-pamoshiri*, which signifies our concept of the world as an interrelated community of all living things. In this new era in which the world is groping towards a redefinition of the international order following the end of the Cold War, we believe "a new partnership" of indigenous and nonindigenous peoples which includes this worldview can make a lasting and valuable contribution to the global community. It is the desire of indigenous peoples to make the future, full of the hopes of all mankind, an even better place. *Iyairaikere.* Thank you very much.

Giichi Nomura is the executive director of the Ainu Association of Hokkaido. The Ainu people are the original people of Japan who now live on the northern island of Hokkaido and the Russian islands of Sakhalin and the Kuriles. They speak Ainu, which is not related to Japanese nor to any other language in the world, yet their language and culture are under pressure from Japan, which has attempted to assimilate them into Japanese society.

LOIS O'DONOGHUE
Chairperson, Aboriginal and Torres Strait Islander
Commission (Pacific Islands)

My name is Lowitja, and I am a member of the
Yankuntjatjara peoples of northern South Australia. I am an aboriginal person. I am accompa-
nied on the platform by George Mye, a Torres Strait Islander.
Together, we stand here before you today, filled with im-
mense pride as representatives of Australia's indigenous
peoples.

Aboriginal culture is the oldest surviving culture in the
world. When in 1770 Captain Cook sighted what was then
described as the Great South Land, we, the first Australians,

had been there for more than fifty thousand years. In 1788, Australia became a British penal colony, a dumping ground for the problems of the British Empire. The British declared Australia *terra nullius*, "no one's land." The indigenous peoples were deemed to have no legal rights to the land on which they had lived and for which they had cared for so long. There were no negotiations, there were no agreements, there were no treaties. There was no recognition that we were a people with distinctive cultures. There was no recognition that Australia's indigenous peoples, with more than five hundred different languages, shared one thing in common—their relationship with the land. That relationship remains central to our very being.

There followed years of oppression and conflict which spread across the continent to dispossess, degrade, and devastate the aboriginal people. It has left a national legacy of unutterable shame. It took the indigenous people of Australia until 1967 to be recognized as Australians under the Australian constitution.

This year we celebrated the twenty-fifth anniversary of that constitutional recognition. We also were given cause to celebrate this year as a result of a decision by the High Court of Australia in what is now known as the Eddie Mabo case. Mabo, a Torres Strait Islander, pursued indigenous rights unrelentingly. As a result the highest court in the land overturned the doctrine of *terra nullius*. After 204 years Australian law has finally recognized that indigenous people did own their land at the time of European settlement in 1788. This recognition is greatly welcome. Indeed, it is more than two centuries overdue. But it remains to be seen what its practical effects will be.

Our land and our culture are the two things in this world that we cherish above all else. We have been dispossessed and dispersed. Our culture has been threatened as a result of colonization. Many of our languages have been lost. Our spiritual beliefs have been ridiculed. We have become marginalized in our own country. In this International Year of the World's Indigenous People we proudly celebrate one thing—

our survival. But our survival has been against overwhelming odds. Aboriginal people have a life expectancy fifteen to twenty years less than other Australians. We have unemployment levels six times that of other workers. We are locked away in prison at a rate twenty-seven times that of white Australians. We are also imprisoned by poverty, poor education, and substance abuse. But we take this opportunity not only to reflect on our past and present status, but to look with hope to our future. We celebrate the fact that we have faced the challenge to our territory, our culture, and our very existence. We have survived.

As part of this celebration we seek to unlock the door to our history, and in doing so we hope to show the world that there is, and always will be, another side to the so-called "discovery" of Australia that wrought havoc upon us. We do not wish to conquer or oppress. Nor indeed do we wish to retaliate for two centuries of injustice. Rather we seek to create a new partnership based upon understanding, cooperation, and goodwill.

The past cannot be changed: our future is in our hands. We will empower ourselves. To all our indigenous brothers and sisters who have suffered and survived the imposition of an alien culture, we offer the hand of friendship and solidarity. To the world we offer a message—share with us a future of peace and hope based upon mutual respect and understanding. Share with us a new partnership based on equality, equal opportunity, and social justice. Share with us a partnership based upon proper knowledge and understanding of each other's culture and heritage and an awareness of the forces that have shaped the indigenous experience. Share with us a partnership to care for the land which nurtures us.

For this partnership to be effective the world must accept that the history of indigenous people has been a history of oppression and the dominance of one race by another. We do not seek your punishment. We simply seek your acknowledgment of the brutality that has occurred, and your recognition of the continuous vitality of our cultures. We need also to accept that our culture is a living and evolving thing that has grown out of an interaction between the past and the present. By giving recognition to this sharing, I believe we can bring a new insight to the many challenges that face the world today. As indigenous people we ask no more than the basic human right of being given the opportunity to determine our own future. Only through self-determination can we begin to address the devastating impact on our people of dispossession and dispersal without consent or compensation. In Australia we are making progress. There is a greater government commitment to self-determination for indigenous peoples. Our education levels are rising sharply. Our cultural achievements are gaining international recognition. But there is so much still to be done.

The next decade in Australia will be significant for indigenous people as we move towards marking the centenary of our federation in the year 2001. It was that federation which brought together the six colonies that now make up the Australian nation. The centenary of that compact holds hope for an equally important new compact—a compact of reconciliation between the country's indigenous and nonindigenous population. That centenary also demands that the Australian constitution be changed to recognize aboriginal and Torres Strait Islander peoples as the continent's original inhabitants. It requires that the land needs and entitlements of Australia's indigenous peoples are appropriately addressed. This will mean seeking land rights not only through proving native title in the courts, not only through improved legislation, but also through the establishment of a National Land Acquisition Fund for those of our people who have been dispossessed.

Finally, the years leading to the centenary of our federation provide an opportunity for Torres Strait Islanders to gain some form of self-governing status over the islands and waters that they hold so dear. The International Year of the World's Indigenous People enables us to embark on a new journey of discovery—a journey that I hope will bring about an understanding of the fundamental nature of our history, and the key to a shared future in justice and equality. It is a journey that we want the aboriginal and Torres Strait Islander peoples of Australia to share with our indigenous brothers and sisters throughout the world.

Lois O'Donoghue is a member of the Yankuntjatjara peoples of northern South Australia, known as Aborigines. She is also the chairperson of the Aboriginal and Torres Strait Islander Commission, an Australian government organization which works with the Aborigines and Torres Strait Islanders.

MORINGE L. PARKIPUNY
KIPOC (Africa)

On behalf of the Masai and the Bemba together with all African indigenous minority peoples, I wish to first of all congratulate the United Nations for your big contributions involving the enormous problems facing the international community today. That also applies to your decision to make 1993 the International Year of the World's Indigenous People. Indigenous sisters and brothers, we are very delighted to meet you again here today, to strengthen the determination to win the restoration of the rights of our peoples, the dignity of our cultures, and our will to protect Mother Earth. Since 1989 the few of us standing here in front have been among the very few indigenous minority people who have been annually attending the United Nations Working Group on Indigenous Populations in Geneva. Through that forum, we have been exposed to many things. We have learned a great deal and established a number of links with fellow members of the worldwide extended family of indigenous people. I therefore take this opportunity to thank our solidarity institutions whose work has enabled us to link up with our sisters and brothers.

In the one hundred years since 1890, the colonial and subsequently the independent African states have waged a continuous attempt to obliterate the cultural identity of our people through policies of assimilation and expropriation of the land—land that constitutes the basis of sustainable survival for us. In Africa there is no generalized practice of genocide against minority peoples. For instance in East Africa, minority peoples of Asian, Arabic, and European descent are free to maintain their lifestyles, languages, religion, and economic ways of life without any intervention by the state. It is specifically indigenous African cultures—which are well known to have languages, lifestyles, and grassroots community-oriented environmental and economic systems that are all profoundly different from those of the mainstream population—which have been actively targeted for total alienation. We are looked down at as evolutionary relics of past primitive ages and considered an outright disgrace to the national image. I hereby appeal to this assembly of the United Nations, to all states in Africa, to abandon the policy that the issues of indigenous peoples do not apply to Africa. Indeed, the continent has a large population of African indigenous minority peoples. It is only as recently as the end of 1980 that it was repeatedly questioned in the debates of the United Nations Working Group on Indigenous Populations whether there were indigenous peoples anywhere in the world. This is the state that Africa is in right now.

In the 1800s, European partitioners carved up Africa into an assortment of forty-eight possessions. This was done in total disregard of the social and ecological boundaries and the economic viability of the territories. Borders were fixed so arbitrarily that many nationalities were sliced into several European domains. For example, Masai land and its people were split between Germany and Britain and divided into three quadrants assigned to the colonial states of Tanganyika, Kenya, and Uganda. These colonial creations were set up without consulting the peoples of the continent. Indigenous African governments were labeled primitive and rigorously attacked, with the objective of total destruction, to enable the conquerors to impose their own systems.

In 1960, the decade in which most of the colonies in Africa were made independent, there was hope that the restoration of the dignity of the peoples of African descent was imminent. However, the leadership of the new states was modeled on patterns drawn in Europe. These leaders have been determined up until now to hold onto their states without altering their boundaries an inch—as if these patterns were the appropriate ones. Indeed, one of the first acts of the founding leaders of African postcolonial states was to sanctify in the Organization of African Unity, the OAU, the habitual boundaries from the era of European colonialism. It deserves to be emphasized that these highly esteemed fathers of independent Africa never consulted the people before taking such an important position.

In addition, the economic systems and other relationships put in place in the colonial era were inherited from Europe and have lingered—with sad consequences. Thirdly, the glaring neglect of the distinct nationalities was perpetuated by the official boundaries drawn in Europe. Despite, or more precisely, in view of the strength of cultural diversity in ways of life, languages, history, and identity of people under their control, the new regimes took an autocratic approach to the promotion of unity. The colonial attempts to destroy African indigenous institutions for social organization, self-determination, and cultural identity were inherited by the independent states who have maintained them. They, in fact, have intensified these attempts, no longer in the name of empire, but in the name of fostering a national unity. African regimes did not proceed soberly, through dialogue with their citizens, to forge remedies to the ailments predictably produced by the malformed birth of the neocolonial state. African governments have invariably and adamantly dismissed even the smallest proposals and portrayed indigenous demands as inspired by antipatriotic sentiments. Needless to state, that was in substance the position previously taken by the colonial regime which perceived Africans' pre-independence aspirations toward self-determination as attitudes of a people still in the age of primitive human civilization who were out to disrupt the rule of law and orderly administration.

The path taken by African unity leaders of these national states, through attempting to obliterate cultural diversity, has proven to be, within the short postcolonial spell of freedom, one of outright disaster. The essential task or mission of the state suffered. It has created simply, across the continent, a quagmire of boundary disputes and thankless wars of nationalities fighting for their right to cultural existence, a right incompatible with the overriding drive for unity. In that scenario, African minority people, outsiders to the mainstream, are being marginalized, deprived of their fundamental freedoms, and having their basic rights violated with impunity through discrimination and prejudice. They are being dispossessed of land and excluded from access to formal education. All these violations of rights are permitted by Africans in the name of promoting national unity, and we are told we are not entitled to belong to the family of indigenous people.

African states have failed to cultivate the available wealth of cultural diversity in the building of a sustainable nation. They, like their European predecessors, tend to see only the negative side of diversity: the tribal hostilities. They refuse to recognize the injustice in the imposition of alien forms of government and of culture, in the destruction of indigenous African values, and the role of these forms of injustice in breeding corruption, nepotism, irresponsibility, and hatred.

The modern African states deny our existence, though we truly exist—the Masai and many others in Tanzania and many, many more all over Africa. We are the states throughout Africa that will blow an irresistible wind of democracy. This wind brings to the fore the question of rights in a civilized society, including our rights as African indigenous minorities.

Moringe L. Parkipuny is a Masai from Kenya. He is also the leader of KIPOC, a national indigenous organization that works for indigenous rights in Kenya.

NOELÍ POCATERRA ULIANI
Movimiento Indio por la Identidad
Nacional (South America)

I invoke the spirit of our ancestors to give the strength and
energy we need so that the voices of our peoples will be
heard. I am a Wayuu indigenous person from Venezuela.
I bring the fraternal greeting of my organization and of the
National Indian Council of Venezuela, the national organization, and of the International Commission of Women of the
World Council of Indigenous Peoples.

I invite you to do some thinking, beginning with these
words: What would mankind be without indigenous peo-

ples—without blood ties with Mother Earth, without forests, without rivers, without birds, butterflies, without the air we breathe? Is it possible that we can so quickly forget the thousands of years of our adaptation to the tropical woods, or to the desert, or to the Arctic polar circle? Is it possible to go on breaking the balance of life? Can man live without his fellow beings, the other living beings of the cosmic community? Therefore, more than an alliance of thought, more than an alliance of intent, we need an alliance with Mother Earth, with its children, and with the Great Spirit.

We must realize once and for all that the destruction of indigenous peoples of the world is also the destruction of mankind. While Western culture speaks of a family of mankind, and holds the family as a basic unit, the indigenous people are not included and are denied the benefits of West-ern society. Among the obstacles to our well-being is that which they call "development" or "progress," which has mistakenly led to unwise state policies, as a result of which indigenous peoples have been condemned to a cultural vacuum, to uprooting, to alcoholism, to prostitution, to repression through birth control, to critical poverty, to the destruction of our economies of coexistence, even deforming our vision of the world and the cultural identity of each people.

In our vision of the world, it is not possible to speak of a family without restoring the role of our elders as the spiritual guide, as the standard for our conduct. We must restore the role of a woman, as a fighter, as a wife, as the reproducer of life, and the key to preserving the identity of our peoples. The young, as our future generations and children, are the continuity of our peoples, and it is they who are our own life. It is not possible in the name of Western science and technology that we should ignore the place of the family and the family of communities of the planet. We cannot ignore Mother Earth and the cosmos, who are the sources of life and have been throughout the history of all peoples.

Hence, we say without guilt that Western science, which came into being to preserve the future, has today become the best instrument to destroy the future. Through advances in technology, it is placing in the hands of a minority the availability of all the natural resources of the planet, when these resources are the property of all the sons of the earth. This can only condemn future generations to war and to exile, generations who within them must feel the aggravation of knowing that this select minority continues to ignore, even in the beginning of the twenty-first century, the positive role of alternative cultures. Yet we continue to be examples and ex- pressions of meaningful spirituality and peaceful existence, and serve as a challenge to Western science, art, and religion.

The International Year of the World's Indigenous People will be meaningful only if the United Nations will also be an expression of the voice and heart of the Indian nations and not only of its member-states. We cannot proceed without expressing this concern. Because I see that the many nations, through all of their empty seats in this hall, are telling us what their solidarity really is and expressing their unwillingness to listen to us. This we fail to understand.

In the case of the Americas, we note that the International Labor Organization Convention No. 169 should be ratified by all of Latin America, and this should be done in the first quarter of 1993, as proof that there is a willingness to listen to the indigenous peoples by adopting the only instrument which is available to us so far under international law. Through this channel, we also request the state of Venezuela and all the states of the Americas to commit themselves to work with indigenous peoples by determining priorities in accordance with the needs of every region of the country and in accordance with every people or nation. This should be one of the United Nations' appeals in the International Year of the World's Indigenous People.

We request of you support for the projects of Progama Minimo of the various American indigenous peoples in 1993 and during the entire decade of the 1990s, which will enable us to welcome with dignity the twenty-first century without giving up our identity or our ancestral status. These development projects for indigenous peoples must start with the family and the local community, and renounce the hegemonic claims of a single world market which will do away with economic and social diversity.

We maintain the need to rearrange American history in its entirety, starting with its first inhabitants, dating back forty thousand years. We are in this process reevaluating our heroes, our chiefs, the peoples of the resistance linked to the historical rights of current aboriginal nations. The indigenous peoples of America and of the world trust that 1993, as our international year, will not become a mere festival which will dash our new hopes.

Nobody can deny that the major problem indigenous people face is the progressive expropriation of their lands and territories. The irrational exploitation of their soil and the consequent destruction and pollution of their lands threatens the world's ecosystems, which sustain the balance of life. This is accelerating due to the delivery of our territories, through privatization, to pay an unpayable external debt that many of the Latin American member-states have burdened themselves with. The United Nations and member-states should be mindful of the warnings of prominent scientists on the risk of the disappearance of the biodiversity of the Orinoco basin, the Amazon, and the Sierra de Perija,* among the many fragile areas necessary for indigenous civilization.

We request special attention to the lack of fundamental human rights for indigenous peoples, who are living under repression in many cases, a repression which is hidden under the banner of state security or the fiction of ecological protection—which largely only facilitates the expropriation of our lands and territories. In Venezuela, the land of indigenous peoples is today crossed by thousands of kilometers of barbed wire, fences, gates, and padlocks.

---

* The Orinoco River and the Sierra de Perija (Guiana highlands), as well as parts of the Amazon basin, are located in Venezuela.

Finally, we would like to state that in Venezuela, as in the rest of the continent, we, the indigenous peoples, live with the systematic violation of our human rights and our rights to our lands, health, bilingual intercultural education, and economic and political equality. There is a progressive environmental degradation which is destroying the indigenous family, lessening our sources of nourishment, affecting our quality of life, and our dignity as people.

We demand that we be heard and that our rights be included in the constitutions of our countries. We therefore appeal to the General Assembly of the United Nations to reflect on the themes I have mentioned so that we will not be left with mere expectations, but with action. This is what the indigenous peoples feel and want. We thank the distinguished representatives and member-states who are here with us in this hall—although we are bound to say that there are only a very small number. We are grateful for your presence. Thank You.

Noelí Pocaterra Uliani is a Wayuu Indian from Venezuela. She is a member of the Movimiento Indio por la Identidad Nacional, a hemispheric Indian organization, and the national Indian organization of Venezuela, the National Indian Council of Venezuela; she is also a member of the International Commission of Women of the World Council of Indigenous Peoples.

TAMATI REEDY
National Maori Congress (Pacific Islands)

I bring greetings and good wishes from the National Congress of Maori of New Zealand. This organization represents forty-five affiliated tribes of the Maori, who are the indigenous people of New Zealand. I speak also as a representative of the second largest tribe of Maori, who will be hosting the first celebration and conference, on January 1, to mark the 1993 International Year of the World's Indigenous People. The focus of our conference is the sovereignty of indigenous people. We, the Maori people, congratulate the United Nations General Assembly for launching this initiative with its theme "Indigenous people—a new partnership."

Unfortunately, as we gather to launch this great event, moves are taking place in New Zealand which will extinguish both treaty and human rights of the Maori people of the land. The New Zealand government last Thursday, December 3, introduced into Parliament a bill called the Treaty of Waitangi Fisheries Claim Settlement Bill. The supposed intent of this bill is to provide the Maori with an economic base at a time when Maori unemployment presently runs between 30 and 40 percent—compared to a national average of 10 percent. Furthermore, the $150 million payment spread over the next three years is to bring to an end all claims pertaining to commercial fisheries that Maori have against the Crown and settle them for all time. In recent court cases by Maori against the Crown, the courts have failed to determine what commercial fishing rights the Maori have. Nevertheless, the Crown has moved to interpret what Maori commercial fishing rights are. The Maori have always claimed 100 percent of the rights to the fisheries around New Zealand, and this claim derives from customary and aboriginal titles validated by a court decision against the Crown in 1986. These rights are further guaranteed under Article II of the Treaty of Waitangi of 1840. This treaty allowed the British Crown and its descendants to settle in New Zealand.

This bill will, therefore, trample not only on treaty rights but also aboriginal rights protected by common law. Furthermore, it will deny basic human rights to Maori people. The bill declares that all claims in respect to commercial fishing, whether founded on rights arising in common law, including customary law, or aboriginal law, including the Treaty of Waitangi, are "Hereby finally settled, fulfilled, satisfied, and discharged." It further rules that no court or tribunal shall have the jurisdiction to inquire into the validity of such claims, the existence of rights, and the interests of Maori as Maori in commercial fishing. Nor can it examine the quantification of these rights or even question the validity of the Deed of Settlement that gave rise to this bill, or even question the accuracy of the benefits to the Maori. With regards to noncommercial fishing rights, those are ours by tradition. This bill consciously strikes out all of these rights also, again with the same explicitness: "Whether founded on rights arising from customary law or aboriginal title, Treaty of Waitangi statute, or otherwise, these rights shall henceforth have no legal effect."

At the introduction of this bill last Thursday, the Crown moved this bill under urgency of the House. In order to avoid the rising protest and opposition from the Maori people, this bill is being denied the normal process of being heard by a select committee of the House. All the Maori members of Parliament protested vigorously at the violation of democratic rights. During the two months preceding the introduction of this bill, the major Maori tribes opposed to this attempt to extinguish treaty and aboriginal rights have appealed in the highest courts of the land, only to be told that the courts cannot interfere with the Crown's right to make laws. Only the Waitangi Tribunal, set up to hear Maori grievances but with powers only to recommend to governments, has declared that the extinguishing of Maori rights is "inconsistent with the Treaty and prejudicial to Maori." The Crown has chosen to ignore the Tribunal. The Maori are disturbed that the Crown has chosen to move to this legislation on the advice of four Maori negotiators—negotiators appointed by the Crown. The Crown further claims that the seventy-five signatures it has collected are sufficient to wipe away the rights of 500,000 individual Maori, including the rights of tribes who oppose or did not sign the Crown's Deed of Settlement.

I bring notice to this great assembly of the United Nations of this act of violation by the government of New Zealand. We are displeased that our country's government, which recently won a place on the United Nations Security Council, should now act in utter violation of the rights of its own minority indigenous people. The fact that it does so on the eve of the 1993 International Year of the World's Indigenous People is remarkable for its callous disregard and insensitivity to indigenous rights. Its action is reminiscent of the land confiscations and denial of Maori rights perpetrated during the colonial period of New Zealand settlement by the British Crown in the last century. We fear the domino effect of this legislation on our land, water, and other cultural rights. I implore on behalf of my people, an investigation by the United Nations Commission on Human Rights of these matters. I also implore on behalf of all indigenous people of the world, their permanent inclusion within the United Nations system. [Maori term used] In English it means the prestige of our people and land remains sacrosanct. We end our message at this great gathering with a song. It asks the eternal question, "Who will care and caress this land, this earth?" It answers with the eternal message, "It is truth, justice, and compassion." [Maori song]

Tamati Reedy is a Maori from New Zealand, otherwise known by its Maori name of Aotearoa. He is a member of the National Maori Congress, an organization that represents forty-five indigenous Maori tribes.

DONALD ROJAS
President, World Council of Indigenous Peoples
(North America)

As a preamble I wish to pay a tribute to all the indigenous heroes who by their strength have enabled us to
be present here on this occasion. I also wish to con- vey
a warm greeting to all the indigenous peoples of the world
—children, young people, men, women, and the elderly. From
this program, through their organization, we announce our
commitment to continue our struggle to seek peaceful solutions
for the exercise of the inherent right to make decisions on our
future. We support every effort for the defense and recognition
of—and respect for—this right of self-determination.

91

With the end of the era of colonialism that celebrated ideas of economic, political, and cultural conquests of our peoples, we welcome the proclamation of the International Year of the World's Indigenous People, a year which the indigenous peoples themselves, through their organized chapters, have forged. We recognize the efforts made by the United Nations and some member-states which have responded favorably to this request, yet we view with great concern that our peoples are not yet considered nations. So it is with pride that we emphasize in this assembly once more that we are present here as peoples. We recognize, too, the important contributions of the United Nations system during the last twenty years, which are reflected in the resolution adopted by the General Assembly, as well as in the opening of the dialogue and possibilities for cooperation with its specialized agencies at a meeting tomorrow. We trust that the meeting will be yet another incentive for developing these new relationships.

We are bound to praise the work of the Working Group on Indigenous Populations, and we anticipate the final version of the Universal Declaration of the Rights of Indigenous Peoples at the eleventh session to be held in 1993. We recommend approval of the Universal Declaration. We encourage activities of the United Nations designed to promote fruitful dialogues among the representatives of the indigenous peoples and states, such as the seminars for the review of economic and social relations held in Geneva in 1989, and forums on self-determination and autonomy in Nuuk, Greenland, in 1991 as well as other activities which were mentioned this morning. Nevertheless, we wish to insist on an appropriate follow-up of the recommendations from these important events.

We would like to suggest that the United Nations consider the establishment of a high-level mechanism such as that of a high commissioner on indigenous issues, which will also include social, cultural, and environmental issues as well as human and indigenous rights. It is also proper to suggest that the United Nations, when planning its programs for indigenous peoples, fully consider the availability of funds needed to ensure the continuous input of the representatives of the indigenous peoples. We reiterate our support for the significant participation of indigenous peoples in all the consultation processes, among them the ratification and implementation of ILO Convention 169. We note with satisfaction the number of countries which have ratified this convention and those who have begun their processes for ratification in the near future.

It is important to enhance the cultural value of all of our cultures and the mutual recognition of diversity. This emphasis will bring about a cultural dialogue seeking to come closer to human harmony and balance. In this respect we appreciate the number of governments which spoke on the subject this morning. We appreciate the governmental organizations for indigenous peoples, and we are prepared to cooperate with them in the spirit of a new relationship in which our decisions will be respected and our participation will be satisfactory. Mother Earth has given us life and sustained us with all its elements. Indigenous peoples are concerned about its deterioration. We offer the world alternatives given us by our ancestors. It will be important for the United Nations to implement sound recommendations for the environment and for sustainable development, particularly the Convention on Biodiversity and the recommendations in Chapter 26 of Agenda 21. The indigenous peoples and our views should be present and appropriately included in the World Conference on Human Rights. It would be ironic if during the International Year of the World's Indigenous People, our affairs were not included in the agenda of the United Nations World Conference.

As we all know, indigenous people are still suffering from the colonial heritage, which historically began and currently supports violations of the human rights of indigenous peoples. We wish to refer to the possibilities open to us in the future. We await with great expectations the creative efforts of indigenous peoples and their activities for 1993. We can face the important challenges of continuing to build on an international indigenous solidarity and seeking to find lasting solutions to maintain life and sustained development for our future. To conclude, we wish to announce some of the important activities contemplated for 1993 by the World Council: the International Conference of Indigenous Peoples in Mexico in May 1993, co-hosted by our organization; the International Conference of Indigenous Women, to be held in Guatemala in the first week of December 1993; and the seventh General Assembly of the World Council of Indigenous Peoples, to be held in Guatemala, from December 6 to 10, 1993.

We will also cooperate with the United Nations and specialized agencies of the international organizations, nongovernmental organizations, and with all organizations of indigenous peoples planning and implementing the activities of the International Year of the Family in 1994; the World Conference on Development and Population, to be held in Cairo, Egypt, in 1994; the World Summit for Social Development; and the World Conference on Women, to be held in China in 1995.

Donald Rojas is the president of the World Council of Indigenous Peoples. This is a worldwide organization that represents the global concerns of indigenous peoples. Based in Canada, the council organizes major forums and meetings on indigenous rights. It also holds large general assemblies around the world, and its sixth General Assembly was held in Norway.

IRJA SEURUJARVI-KARI
Nordic Saami Council (Northern Europe)

The Nordic Saami Council, which represents the Saami Nation of Finland, Norway, Sweden, and Russia, welcomes the proclamation of 1993 as the International Year of the World's Indigenous People, and we express the hope and expectation that the International Year will serve to further the development of cooperation and respect for human rights which are necessary for indigenous survival.

The charter of the United Nations talks about the peoples of this world, and international human rights law clearly establishes the fundamental rule of equality between all individuals, and between all national and ethnic groups in the enjoyment of human rights and fundamental freedoms. Discrimination is prohibited, and a number of international instruments provide for special rights and special measures in order to guarantee equal enjoyment for underprivileged groups. Indigenous peoples are entitled to equal enjoyment and protection under these rules. In addition, we have the right of self-determination, as provided for in the international instruments on human rights, and the right to continued existence as distinct peoples. These rights must be implemented with due consideration to all the principles of public and international law. Autonomy and self-determination are essential components of these international implementation efforts.

The International Labor Conference of 1989 concerned itself with indigenous and tribal peoples in independent countries, and the ILO Convention No. 169 has now been ratified by several countries, among them Norway. The World Bank has also adopted operational guidelines for relations with indigenous peoples. In ever-increasing numbers, elements of the United Nations are addressing the situation of indigenous peoples, including the Commission on Human Rights, its subcommission the Treaty Implementation Bodies, and various seminars and workshops. The focal point of these activities continues to be the United Nations Working Group on Indigenous Populations, under the able leadership of Madam Erica Daes. The Working Group has made good progress but has yet to complete its main task of drafting a new declaration on the rights and freedoms of indigenous peoples. We believe strongly that keeping the Working Group open and accessible, as it is to all the parties concerned, should continue uninterrupted until meaningful and substantive standards emerge from the deliberations and with the consent of all of the participants. The substance is more important to us than the date of adoption, and we trust the Working Group to finalize the draft declaration before sending it to its parent bodies.

The Working Group also has the mandate to review developments relating to situations facing indigenous peoples worldwide. We believe this task is an important one for both implementation of existing rights and for identification of issues to be addressed by the declaration. We are happy to report that the Nordic countries have consistently been active participants in the Working Group, and, along the same lines, we encourage the Working Group to continue its considerations on Nordic issues, including, in particular, the land rights of the Saami Nation in Russia and Sweden.

The links between human rights, democracy, and sustainable development have emerged with increasing clarity from the work of organizations on indigenous peoples' issues. These links are reflected in the work of the groups, but they should also be developed in the operational work of the United Nations' systems. We are content that the International Labor Organization has repeatedly had international coordination meetings in this field, and we endorse the emphasis which is placed on the development and partnership aspects of the program of the International Year. In order to achieve these goals, indigenous peoples and their organizations must have the opportunity to participate effectively in all the relevant activities at all levels.

For indigenous representatives to speak in this distinguished General Assembly has obvious symbolic value, and we appreciate the invitation. It means very much to us. The occasion will, however, only gain real and lasting value if it is the beginning of true partnership based on goodwill and cooperation, with roots firmly planted in respect for human rights, equality, and dignity for all. It is in this spirit that we have come here today, and it is in this spirit that we look forward to the future.

Irja Seurujarvi-Kari is a member of the Nordic Saami Council, an organization that represents Saami people of Finland, Norway, Sweden, and Russia. The Saami are known for their management of the vast reindeer herds that migrate across and near the Arctic Circle. Fallout from the nuclear accident in Chernobyl devastated the reindeer herds by contaminating lichen, their main food source.

MARY SIMON
Inuit Circumpolar Conference (Arctic)

The United Nations plays a crucial role in setting needed international standards. Your persistent efforts in monitoring the members of the international community and encouraging respect for the human rights of all peoples are vital. Indigenous people firmly support the overall objective and work of the United Nations. I am Mary Simon, an Inuit leader from Nunavut in northern Canada. I am speaking on behalf of the Inuit, the Cree of James Bay, nonstatus and off-reserve Indians, and Metis, representing a majority of the indigenous peoples of Canada and the International Organization of Indigenous Resource Development.*

Indigenous peoples from every region of the globe are among the most vulnerable and exploited societies. We, perhaps more than any other peoples in the world, urgently need the international protection that the United Nations can provide. Although the theme of the International Year is a new partnership, the reality we face is not one of partnership or cooperation but rather exclusion and marginalization. Dispossession of lands and resources, racial discrimination, and other violations of our most fundamental rights still scar and ravage the lives of indigenous peoples in both developing and developed countries. On the eve of 1993, a number of state governments still refuse to recognize our collective and individual rights as peoples. Our rights are inseparable from our cultures, way of life, and our relationship to our land and territories. We are people with the same rights as all peoples. To deny this is to deny who we are. We are no longer merely objects of international law, we are subjects of international law.

Finally the international community has started to take meaningful steps to address the urgent human rights concerns of indigenous peoples. In 1989, the International Labor Organization adopted the Indigenous and Tribal Peoples' Convention, or Convention 169, which is intended to provide international protection to indigenous tribal peoples. With a mandate from this General Assembly and with the direct participation of indigenous peoples, the United Nations Working Group of Indigenous Populations is drafting a Universal Declaration on the Rights of Indigenous Peoples. To be effective, this document must not become the lowest common denominator of existing domestic law. Instead, it should conform to the status, rights, and perspectives of indigenous peoples

* The Metis are mixed-blood Indians of French ancestry, status Indians are those nations that are not recognized by the Canadian government. Off-reserve Indians are Indians who do not live on "reserves," the Canadian term for Indian reservations. The Cree are a large family of Indian nations in Canada. The Inuit were until recently called Eskimos and are distinct from Indians.

themselves, whose concerns must now be addressed by the United Nations. To advance this effort, we need individuals like Dr. Erica Daes, chairperson of the Working Group. Dr. Daes is an untiring advocate on behalf of our rights at the United Nations.

We believe that the urgent concerns of millions of indigenous peoples throughout the world can no longer remain a footnote to the overall work of the United Nations. At the very least the rights of indigenous peoples must finally gain a place on the formal agenda of the Commission on Human Rights. More fundamentally, we recommend the following: that the institutional framework of the United Nations be appropriately strengthened to recognize the increasing importance of the issues affecting indigenous peoples; that a permanent advisory body within the United Nations be created, made up of representatives of indigenous peoples themselves. The struggle against apartheid in South Africa has benefited from such an advisory committee. This is a model we should seek to emulate. I emphasize that we cannot rely entirely upon domestic law to provide the necessary protection and promotion of our human rights and fundamental freedoms—these include our collective and individual rights. We must go beyond the protection provided for minorities under Article 27 of the International Covenant on Civil and Political Rights, which is simply inadequate.

Indigenous peoples must have the right to consent to development on indigenous land. Indigenous peoples are often the first to suffer the adverse social and environmental effects of ill-conceived development projects. The Cree of James Bay have come here suffering from the effects of massive flooding of their territory in northern Quebec,* as are other people here who have had clear-cut forestry on their lands. Agreements and treaties between indigenous peoples and states must be

---

* From the James Bay hydroelectric project, known as James Bay I (which is largely complete) and II (which is vigorously being contested). These projects form the largest industrial development in the history of North America.

fully respected under international law. Such treaties include modern land claims agreements. Indigenous treaties were not signed only as domestic instruments; they must not be turned into domestic instruments after the fact.

Respect of our right to self-determination is paramount. Our right to subsistence, our rights to benefit from our own resources, our rights to self-government—many of our fundamental rights are contingent upon respect for our right to self-determination. The Inuit of Resolute Bay and Grise Fjord in Canada have been victims of forced relocation to support Canada's claim to northern sovereignty, and as a result, they suffered numerous violations of their human rights. The government of Canada owes an apology and compensation to these people of the high Arctic.* The pain and suffering of these Inuit families is further compounded by the Canadian government's attempt to deny this injustice. The indigenous peoples in Quebec are now threatened by the possible secession of Quebec from Canada. The indigenous rights of self-determination must take precedence under these circumstances.

On a more positive note the Inuit of Nunavut have moved closer to controlling their own lives through a recent comprehensive land claims agreement and a political accord on the division of the Northwest Territory. And the Metis Nation has agreed to a legislative accord with the government, the Metis Nation Accord, which must now be processed. During the Canadian constitutional negotiations, the recognition of the inherent right to self-government for all aboriginal peoples by the Canadian government was a historic breakthrough. Although the combined provisions of the Charlottetown accords were not ratified, the self-government provisions gained broad support among Canadians. Canada must now conclude constitutionally binding self-government agreements with aboriginal peoples.

Today, Rigoberta Menchú, an indigenous person from

* The Inuit were relocated in two stages, in 1953 and 1955, from Resolute Bay to Grise Fjord. Ostensibly this was done by the Canadian government for their welfare, though the Inuit obviously disagree.

Guatemala, has received the Nobel Peace Prize for her courage and determination. We add our heartfelt tribute to her remarkable and ongoing efforts. In closing, our presence today before the General Assembly is not an isolated event. We call upon the General Assembly to go beyond the relatively unsubstantial resolution which has been proposed and to endorse a plan of action which will address indigenous issues for the next decade. In addition, much more funding is required at both the international level and for state programs.

Mary Simon is a member of the Inuit Circumpolar Conference, an organization that represents Inuit peoples in Canada, Alaska, and Russia. The Inuit peoples, known as Eskimos, are famous for their ability to survive in the frozen northern lands. Recent attempts by the United States to turn the Inuit from self-governing villagers into shareholders of native corporations, and give up the sovereign rights other Native Americans are entitled to in the United States, was a primary impetus to establishing the conference. Mary Simon has been a leader of the struggle by the Cree and Inuit protesting the James Bay hydroelectric project in Canada, a project which would severely damage the environment of a pristine wilderness the size of France.

ANDERSON MUUTANG URUD

Sarawak Indigenous Peoples' Alliance
(Southeast Asia)

I am from the Kelabit tribe of Sarawak, Malaysia, and I speak on behalf of my people. I want to thank the International Federation of Human Rights for inviting me to speak before this important and honorable audience. On behalf of the Dayak peoples of Sarawak, Malaysia, and my unrepresented brothers and sisters in the southeast Asian nations, in Indonesia, the Philippines, West Papua, and Thailand, I want to thank the United Nations for making 1993 the International Year of the World's Indigenous People.

It is my peoples' hope that the sun has finally risen over the green mountains after its long battle with the cold night. I share this hope with my indigenous brothers and sisters who have come here from all parts of the world. This International Year of the World's Indigenous People gives us hope, but at the same time, we must all ask ourselves if this year is receiving enough support and enough funding. I hope that a serious commitment to this new partnership is forthcoming from the United Nations.

Sarawak, which is in the state of Malaysia, located on the island of Borneo, is less than 2 percent of the size of Brazil, yet it currently produces almost two-thirds of the world's supply of tropical timber. Nowhere in the world is the primary forest disappearing faster than it is in Sarawak. Even if the current rate of logging were immediately reduced by one-half, all of the primary forests in Sarawak would be destroyed by the year 2000. In areas that are logged the fish, wild animals, and medicinal plants disappear. The trees, which bear the fruit which feeds the wild pigs, are cut down for timber. The pigs just disappear and with them vanishes the main source of meat for our peoples. Many of us are now hungry. When trees and vines with poisonous barks are felled and find their way into the streams, they kill all of the fish. Mud from the eroded land pollutes the rivers, leaving us with disease and destroying our source of drinking water. Even when we mark our burial grounds, the logging companies bulldoze through them with no regard for our feelings. Hundreds of graveyards have been destroyed in this way. When we complain about the destruction, they sometimes offer us a small sum of money as compensation, but this is an insult to us. How can we accept money that is traded for the bodies of our ancestors?

The government says that it is bringing us progress and development, but the only development that we see is the dusty logging roads and the relocation camps. This so-called progress means only starvation, dependence, helplessness, and the destruction of our culture and demoralization of our people. The government says it is creating jobs for our people, but these jobs will disappear along with the forest. In ten years the jobs will all be gone, and the forest, which has sustained us for thousands of years, will be gone with them. And why do we need jobs? My father and my grandfather did not ask the government for jobs. They were never unemployed. They lived from the land and from the forests. It was a good life. We had much leisure time, and yet we were never hungry or in need. These company jobs take men away from their families and from our communities for months at times. They are breaking apart the vital links which have held our families and our communities together for generations. These jobs bring our people into the consumer economy, for which our people are not prepared.

The Penan, the Kelabit, and the other Dayak peoples view the forest as our home. When we see an intruder enter into our home, we must defend what is ours. That is why we have been protesting peacefully for so long against the loggers, against the system that perpetuates this. That is why when these protests fell on deaf ears, we began to blockade logging roads. Since 1987, hundreds of our people have been arrested and imprisoned for taking part in these peaceful blockades. An old man once asked a policeman, why is it that he could not blockade a road on his own land. The policeman told him that Yayasan Sarawak, a company which has been given the license to log the forests, by law owns the land. This is what the old man replied: "Who is this Yayasan Sarawak? If he really owns the land, why have I never met him in the forest during my hunting trips over the last sixty years?"

A woman I know who has seven children once came to me and said, "This logging is like a big tree that has fallen on my chest. I often wake in the middle of the night, and my husband and I talk endlessly about the future of our children. I always ask myself 'When will it end?' " For defending our way of life, we have been called "greenies, pirates, terrorists, and traitors." I have been put in prison and into solitary confinement. Yesterday the government of Sarawak renewed a six-month warrant of arrest ordering my detention until next year. Our lives are threatened by company goons. Our women are being raped by loggers who invade our villages. While the companies get rich from our forests, we are condemned to live in poverty and eventual genocide.

Our situation is not unlike that of a child who has fallen into the fast-flowing river and cannot swim. The child cries out, extending its arms to someone for help. If no one lends a hand, the child will certainly drown. It is for this reason that I call upon the United Nations, the government of governments, to do its utmost to assist all indigenous peoples who are threatened by their own government. This body must urge member-states to restore immediately the human and economic rights of the weakest and the most vulnerable of the world's peoples. I propose that the United Nations send peacekeeping observers where indigenous peoples have conflicts with their own governments, and I fully support the proposals that have been put forward by the distinguished delegates and representatives of the indigenous people that have spoken before me.

Must people die before you respond? Must there be war and blood running in the streets or in the jungles before the United Nations will come to a people's assistance? Even though we are desperate, our people have avoided violence. We have used only peaceful methods of protest. Why does this organization which is dedicated to peace not listen to the pleas of peaceful people? I say to my country and to other developing countries, that in our race to modernize, we must respect the rich ancient cultures and traditions of our peoples. We must not blindly follow the model of progress invented by Western civilization. We may envy the industrialized world for its wealth, but we must not forget that this world was bought at a very high price. The rich world suffers from so much stress, pollution, violence, poverty, and spiritual emptiness. The riches of indigenous communities lie not in money or commodities but in community, in tradition, and the sense of belonging to a special place.

The world is rushing towards a single culture. We should

pause and reflect on the beauty of diversity. I bring to the attention of my government that it should stop its efforts to assimilate us into the culture of the dominant group. Let 1993, the International Year of the World's Indigenous People, bring a year of peace and hope, a year of restoration of the bleeding forests and of our threatened cultures. Let this year carry its message into the forests of Borneo, to the woman who weeps, praying in the night that the beds of her children will not be like hers.

Anderson Muutang Urud is a member of the Kelabit tribe of Malaysia and a leader of the Sarawak Indigenous Peoples' Alliance, a national indigenous organization. Deforestation, through logging, is severely impacting the way indigenous people in Malaysia live. Attempts by the Kelabits and the Dayaks to redress the taking of their lands has led to serious human rights abuses by the Malaysian government against indigenous peoples.

DAVI YANOMAMI
Yanomami (Brazil)

I t is a great honor for the Yanomami people, and for all the forest peoples of the Amazon, for me to be speaking to the General Assembly of the United Nations at the official opening of the International Year of the World's Indigenous People. Their history over the centuries has not been different from our own. It is the first time that I am speaking at a global forum, and I am grateful for the opportunity. My presence here expresses the spirit of the "new partnership" between peoples proclaimed by the General Assembly.

I remember well my first visit to the United Nations. In April 1991, I was received by then Secretary General Javier

Perez de Cuellar. I explained to him the aggression my people were suffering from, and he promised to pay special attention to our case. Later, he wrote to former Brazilian President Fernando Collor de Mello, expressing his concern. His intervention was important for us. After President Collor received the communications, he started to pay more attention to Indians and their rights.

It was the beginning of a process that did us much good. It led, first, to President Collor's courageous decision in November 1991 to create a single reserve for us covering our traditional lands. In May 1992, just before the Earth Summit held in Rio de Janeiro, it led to the ratification—also by President Collor—of the demarcation of our 96,650-square-kilometer reserve.

For a while, it seemed as if we had turned back the wave of aggressors who were infecting us with their diseases and destroying the land of our ancestors. We had obtained full legal rights to our traditional lands, and the Brazilian government's Indian agency, FUNAI, with the Federal Police, was expelling the invaders from our lands. By July, there were just 200 or 300 *garimpeiros* (gold miners) on our land, compared to 40,000 at the worst moment for us, at the end of 1990.

In recent weeks, however, we have been facing new problems. Because of the political difficulties in Brasilia and the suspension and resignation of President Collor, government activities have come to a standstill. The *garimpeiros* are taking advantage, invading our lands once again. Ferryboats are carrying them over the Calaburi River in the western part of our lands. And in the east, many small planes are flying into our lands from the airport in Boa Vista, capital of the state of Roraima, and from illegal airstrips on nearby ranches. There are now at least 8,000 *garimpeiros* back on our lands. The *garimpeiros* are constantly flying over our lands, scaring us with the sound of their planes. They are threatening the people who work with us, healthcare providers, and FUNAI employees. In some areas, the miners are persuading some of my people to work for them, tempting them with false promises.

At the same time, we are getting ill. Malaria is out of control.

My relatives are dying. We are fearful of another epidemic, like the one between 1987 and 1991, that killed so many of us.*

All our problems have the same cause: lack of political will on the part of the Brazilian federal government. Though the current minister of justice under President Itamar Franco has promised to help, we have as yet received nothing. We need the government to state clearly that our lands are our lands alone. We need the government to provide money so that FUNAI and the Federal Police can expel the invaders, and so that we can receive white man's medicine to heal us of the white man's diseases.

In our difficulty, we turn once again to the United Nations. We ask the new Secretary General, Boutros Boutros-Ghali, if he will help us like his predecessor. We ask him to ask President Franco to send us the help we urgently need. We also call on the International Labor Organization to investigate the conditions in which the *garimpeiros* work. The mining activity taking place on our lands is not only illegal, it is also harmful to the miners themselves. Many of them are held like slaves. Like us, they also are victims of the greed of the handful of men who control the gold trade.

We are doing all we can to help ourselves. To protect us from the white man's diseases, we are setting up our own health project. In my region of the Yanomami land, the river valleys of the Demini, Balawau, and Toototobi, we have twenty-four villages and a population of 1,048. With the help of the governmental agencies in Canada, Germany, Great Britain, and Switzerland, and nongovernmental organizations in Great Britain, Holland, Norway, and Brazil, we are setting up a health project that should reach them all. It is the "new partnership" among peoples.

Finally, I wish to give you a message from *Omam. Omam* is the creator of the Yanomami and the creator of the *shaboris*, who are our shamans. The *shaboris* have all the knowledge, and

---

* About 1,500 Yanomami died out of a population of less than 10,000.

they have sent us to deliver their message to the United Nations: stop the destruction, stop taking minerals from under the ground, and stop building roads through forests. Our word is to protect nature, the wind, the mountains, the forest, the animals, and this is what we want to teach you.

The leaders of the rich, industrialized world think that they are the owners of the world. But the *shaboris* are the ones that have true knowledge. They are the real First World. And if their knowledge is destroyed, then the white people too will die. It will be the end of the world. This is what we want to avoid.

Davi Yanomami is a member of the Yanomami tribe of Brazil and Venezuela. Among the largest of the Amazonian tribes, they are well known for their abilities to successfully struggle for their lands and culture. They have been plagued by new diseases imported by anthropologists, as well as gold miners, loggers, and ranchers.

THOMAS BANYACYA
Hopi elder (North America)

First, I would like to ask that everyone of you stand up for a few minutes. I am going to offer a short prayer, and our brother Oren Lyons of the Six Nations will make an announcement as our way of delivering a message to Indian peoples anywhere in this country.

[Oren Lyons, Faithkeeper of the Haudenosaunee and the first speaker of the day, then proceeded to give three shouts. The shouts were a spiritual announcement to the Great Spirit of the presence of the people assembled and the intention to give a message of spiritual importance.

Thomas Banyacya then sprinkled cornmeal next to the podium of the General Assembly and made a brief remark in Hopi that translates as follows: "Hopi spiritual leaders had an ancient prophecy that someday world leaders would gather in a Great House of Mica with rules and regulations to solve world problems without a war. I am amazed to see the prophecy has come true and here you are today! But only a handful of United Nations delegates are present to hear the *Motee Sinom* (First People) from around the world who have spoken here today."]

My name is Banyacya of the Wolf, Fox, and Coyote clans and I am a member of the Hopi sovereign Nation. Hopi in our language means a peaceful, kind, gentle, truthful people. The traditional Hopi follows the spiritual path that was given to us by *Masau'u*, the Great Spirit. We made a sacred covenant to follow his life plan at all times, which includes the responsibility of taking care of this land and life for his divine purpose. We have never made treaties with any foreign nation, including the United States, but for many centuries we have honored this sacred agreement. Our goals are not to gain political control, monetary wealth, or military power, but rather to pray and to promote the welfare of all living beings and to preserve the world in a natural way. We still have our ancient sacred stone tablets and spiritual religious societies which are the foundations of the Hopi way of life. Our history says our white brother should have retained those same sacred objects and spiritual foundations.

In 1948, all traditional Hopi spiritual leaders met and spoke of things I felt strongly were of great importance to all people. They selected four interpreters to carry their message, of which I am the only one still living today. At that time I was given a sacred prayer feather by the spiritual leaders. I made a commitment to carry the Hopi message of peace and deliver warnings from prophecies known since the time the previous world was destroyed by flood and our ancestors came to this land.

My mission was also to open the doors of the Great House

of Mica to native peoples. The elders said to knock four times. This commitment was fulfilled when I delivered a letter and the sacred prayer feather I had been given to John Washburn in the Secretary General's office in October 1991.

At the meeting in 1948, Hopi leaders—eighty, ninety, and even one hundred years old—explained that the Creator made the First World in perfect balance, where humans spoke a common language. But humans turned away from moral and spiritual principles. They misused their spiritual powers for selfish purposes. They did not follow nature's rules. Eventually, their world was destroyed by the sinking of land and the separation of land which you would call major earthquakes. Many died, and only a small handful survived.

Then this handful of peaceful people came into the Second World. There they repeated their mistakes, and the world was destroyed by freezing, which you call the great Ice Age.

The few survivors entered the Third World. That world lasted a long time, and as in previous worlds, the people spoke one language. The people invented many machines and conveniences of high technology, some of which have not been seen yet in this age. They even had spiritual powers that they used for good. They gradually turned away from natural laws and pursued only material things, and finally only gambled while they ridiculed spiritual principles. No one stopped them from this course, and the world was destroyed by the Great Flood that many nations still recall in their ancient history or in their religions.

The elders said that again only a small group escaped and came to this Fourth World, where we now live. Our world is in terrible shape again even though the Great Spirit gave us different languages and sent us to the four corners of the world; and told us to take care of the earth and all that is in it.

The Hopi ceremonial rattle represents Mother Earth. The line running around it is a time line and indicates that we are in the final days of the prophecy. What have you as individuals, as nations, and as the world body been doing to take care of this earth? In the earth today, humans poison their own food, water, and air with pollution. Many of us, including the children, are left to starve. Many wars are still being fought. Greed and concern for material things is a common disease.

In the Western Hemisphere, our homeland, many original native people are landless, homeless, starving, and have no medical help.

The Hopi knew humans would develop many powerful technologies that would be abused. In this century we have seen World War I and World War II, in which the predicted Gourd of Ashes, which you call the atomic bomb, fell from the sky with great destruction. Many thousands of people were destroyed in Hiroshima and Nagasaki.

For many years there has been great fear and the danger of World War III. The Hopi believed the Persian Gulf War was the beginning of World War III, but it was stopped and the worst weapons of destruction were not used. This is now a time to weigh the choices for our future. We do have a choice. If you, the nations of this earth create another great war, the Hopi believe we humans will burn ourselves to death with ashes. That is why the spiritual elders stress strongly that the United Nations fully open the door for native spiritual leaders to speak as soon as possible.

Nature herself does not speak with a voice that we can easily understand. Neither can the animals and birds we are threatening with extinction talk to us. Who in this world can speak for nature and the spiritual energy that creates and flows through all life? In every continent are human beings who are like you but who have not separated themselves from the land and from nature. It is through their voice that nature can speak to us. You have heard the voices and many messages from the four corners of the world today. I have studied comparative religion, and I think in your own nations and cultures you have an understanding of the consequences of living out of balance with nature and spirit. The native peoples of the world have seen and spoken to you about the destruction of their lives and homelands, the ruination of nature, and the desecration of their sacred sites. It is time the United Nations used its rules to investigate these occurrences and stop them now.

The Four Corners area of the Hopi is bordered by four sacred mountains. The spiritual center within is a sacred site that our prophecies say will have a special purpose in the future—for mankind to survive—and now should be left in its natural state. All nations must protect this spiritual center. The Hopi and all original native people hold the land in balance by prayer, fasting, and performing ceremonies. Our spiritual elders still hold the land in the Western Hemisphere in balance for all living beings, including humans. No one should be relocated from their sacred homelands in this hemisphere or anywhere in the world. Acts of forced relocation, such as Public Law 93-531* in the United States, must be repealed.

The United Nations stands on our native homeland. The United Nations talks about human rights, equality, and justice, and yet the native people have never had a real opportunity to speak to this assembly since its establishment. It should be the mission of your nations and this assembly to use your power and rules to examine and work to cure the damage people have done to this earth and to each other. Hopi elders know that was your mission, and they wait to see whether you will act on it now.

Nature, the first people, and the spirit of our ancestors are giving you loud warnings. You see increasing floods, more damaging hurricanes, hailstorms, climate changes, and earthquakes—as our prophecies said would come. Even animals and birds are warning us with strange changes in their behavior, such as the beaching of whales. Why do animals act like they know about the earth's problems and most humans act

---

* The Navajo-Hopi Land Settlement Act of 1974. It mandated the removal of thousands of Navajo and hundreds of Hopi from their homes, ostensibly to resolve conflicting claims to land between the two groups, but largely as a result of pressure by mining and energy industries. Known as the Big Mountain issue, because many of the Navajo resisters to relocation lived and continue to live in that region of northeastern Arizona, the forced relocations have resulted in significant hardship and suffering to the Navajos, who were among the most traditional and self-sustaining members of their nation.

like they know nothing? If we humans do not wake up to the warnings, the Great Purification will come to destroy this world—just as the previous worlds were destroyed.

[Thomas Banyacya and Oren Lyons held up a large canvas with pictographs from Hopiland.]

This rock drawing shows part of the Hopi prophecy. There are two paths. The first, with high technology but separate from natural and spiritual laws, leads to these jagged lines representing chaos. The lower path is one that remains in harmony with natural law. Here we see a line that represents a choice, like a bridge joining the paths. If we return to spiritual harmony and live from our hearts, we can experience a paradise in this world. If we continue only on this upper path, we will come to destruction.

It is up to all of us, as children of Mother Earth, to clean up this mess before it is too late. The elders request that, during this International Year of the World's Indigenous People, the United Nations keep that door open for spiritual leaders from the four corners of the world to come to speak to you—for more than a few minutes—as soon as possible. The elders also request that eight investigative teams visit the native areas of the world to observe and tell the truth about what is being done and stop these nations from moving in this self-destructive direction.

If any of your leaders want to learn more about the spiritual vision and power of the elders, I invite you to come to Hopiland and sit down with our real spiritual leaders in their sacred kivas, where they will reveal the ancient secrets of survival and balance.

I hope that all members of this assembly that know the spiritual way will not just talk about it, but in order to have real peace and harmony, will really follow what it says across the United Nations wall: "They shall beat their swords into plowshares and study war no more." Let us together do that now.

[The night before the presentation by native people from

around the world to the General Assembly, there was a total eclipse of the moon over New York City, and the sky was clear. The day after the presentation by Mr. Banyacya and the other native spokespersons, heavy rain and strong winds raged above New York, toppling trees on the grounds of the United Nations. What came was the worst flooding in New York City's memory. Major highways were closed, some houses were washed away by the sea, and the United Nations itself experienced flooding of its lower subfloors, forcing the closing of its heating and air-conditioning system. United Nations' personnel were sent home, and many businesses in Manhattan closed for the day. For many of the indigenous people gathered, these occurrences were more than merely coincidental.]

Thomas Banyacya is a Hopi elder from Hotevilla, in the northern Arizona desert. Hotevilla is among the most traditional Hopi villages, having been founded at the turn of the century as a response to the changing ways of the other Hopi villages. Banyacya was chosen to be one of four messengers to prepare the way for the United Nations to receive the Hopi prophecy, a prophecy that had to be delivered at the United Nations. He is still attempting to get this prophesy delivered.

EPILOGUE
Oren Lyons

December 10, 1992, was historic for indigenous peoples of the world. Twenty indigenous leaders addressed the General Assembly from the podium for the first time in the history of the United Nations, intitiating the International Year of the World's Indigenous People. It was a victory of great consequence. This day vindicated and consecrated the work, perseverance, and spirit of all those indigenous delegates, international lawyers, and nongovernmental organizations (NGOs) who attended the United Nations Geneva conferences on racial discrimination, the pro- tection of minorities, and the human rights of indigenous peoples in Geneva beginning in 1977.

Secretary General Boutros Boutros-Ghali delivered a serious and supportive address that gave hope and raised expectations for the coming International Year. At that time he announced the appointment of 1992 Nobel Peace Prize Laureate Rigoberta Menchú Tum as goodwill ambassador for the International Year of the World's Indigenous People.

The decision to designate this International Year and the support of the Secretary General were a marked contrast to our first conference in Geneva in 1977. That first visit elicited all the stereotypical reactions of an uninformed world public towards indigenous peoples—Native American delegates were referred to as "Red Indians," for example. Those who did not participate in those formative years may say there has been little or no movement for the advancement of indigenous peoples, but in fact there have been extraordinary advances, especially within the United Nations.

I remember in 1973 we "Red Indians" were not allowed to cross First Avenue across from the United Nations in the cause of supporting the Lakota people who were suffering United States military oppression at Wounded Knee, South Dakota. Twenty years later, it was a Lakota spiritual leader, Arvol Looking Horse, who gave the opening prayer and stood with Apache representive Ola Cassadore as I delivered the opening address of indigenous representatives to the General Assembly.

Then again, one could say there has been no change, and that would also be true. Attitudes of racism still prevail around the world. Certainly the amount raised by the Voluntary Fund for the 1993 International Year of the World's Indigenous People reflected, at the least, disrespect, lack of interest, and neglect on the part of the member-states. Two weeks before the opening day (December 10, 1992) there was only $40,000 in the fund. This was an insult to indigenous peoples and an embarrassment to member-states of the United Nations. Intense lobbying produced an additional $300,000 by opening day. That figure contrasts with the $33 million worth of "indigenous project proposals submitted to the Secretariat established for the International Year of the World's Indigenous People.

Indigenous people have brought into the United Nations forum an honesty and directness that have been both refreshing and challenging to the subtle diplomacy of United Nations politics. We have confronted, affronted, and offended powerful member-states, sometimes with serious consequences to our delegates, including death.

One could say that the United Nations did not escape some warning and retribution, when the last speaker of that historic December day, Hopi elder Thomas Banyacya, invoked the powers of the natural forces, and New York City experienced the worst storm of this century, with great winds and floods that covered the roofs of cars on East River Drive, flooded the subway systems for the first time, and joined the East River with the Hudson River in Lower Manhattan. Coincidence or invocation, no one can deny that the experience of these powerful forces reminded us that we do not control nature—dramatically amplifying the messages delivered by the indigenous peoples to the United Nations General Assembly.

The June 1993 World Conference on Human Rights in Vienna produced several initiatives regarding indigenous peoples. The conference adopted a resolution to extend the 1993 International Year of the World's Indigenous People to the Decade of Indigenous Peoples and recommended that Secretary General Boutros Boutros-Ghali "consider establishing as soon as possible a permanent forum for indigenous peoples in the United Nations system." We add to this the need for special accreditation for indigenous peoples to the United Nations.

The efforts to complete the international standards on the rights of indigenous peoples commenced with meetings in Geneva beginning in July by the Working Group on Indigenous Populations. These historic meetings came out of the vision and work of Augusto Williamson-Diaz, who initally shepherded the process and idea through the bureaucratic maze of the United Nations in the early seventies.

Indigenous peoples reached their second plateau when the Working Group on Indigenous Populations was officially instituted within its parent body, the Subcommission on Prevention of Discrimination and Protection of Minorities within the Commission on Human Rights in 1982.

In 1985 Erica-Irene A. Daes became chair of the Working Group and has held that position ever since. Her leadership has been at times passionate, dictatorial, artful, shrewd, manipulative, sagacious, and tough. She has always exhibited her great experience and brilliance in dealing with the often hostile member-states and the inexperience of indigenous nations and peoples new to the intricacies of the United Nations. The diplomatic and political language and protocol of the United Nations is a law unto itself, and it is essential that we understand and learn it. We demand full recognition as peoples and nations—we expect nothing less.

In 1977 Robert "Tim" Coulter (who became director of the Indian Law Resource Center) and the International Indian Treaty Council collaborated to bring indigenous delegations to Geneva. Ann Maytag of the Maytag Foundation was instrumental in furnishing financial support for this event. Her assistance ensured the attendance and leadership of traditional indigenous nations and peoples, including the Haudenosaunee delegation of 26 representatives, with 18 chiefs and clan mothers. There were about 148 delegates at this initial meeting.

Credit and recognition should be given to those inspired and dedicated lawyers (native and non-native) and to the many other individuals who have contributed so greatly through the years of political and diplomatic battles within the United Nations structure as we forged a process of recognition and policy for indigenous peoples.

The Working Group on Indigenous Populations' meeting of July 1993 drew 124 indigenous delegations from around the world, 24 observers from United Nations member-states, and 74 NGOs—totaling over 500 participants.

There were large delegations from Australia and New Zealand representing aboriginal and Maori peoples. The Haudenosaunee delegation combined with the Lakota, Teton, Sioux, and Cree nations, maintained the continuum of the traditional indigenous leadership that inspired the first meeting in 1977. An informal show of hands provided the information that only five individual delegates from that first meeting were attending this eleventh session of the Working Group, two from North America and three from South America. The eleventh session produced this final draft, and it is a strong draft that includes group rights and self-determination but unfortunately no reference to sovereignty. The draft declaration addresses issues of lands, territories, coastal waters, and the environment. There are strong references to spiritual and intellectual property and the recognition of treaties as international instruments. The full text of this draft declaration is included in this book (Appendix B).

The most dramatic event of the United Nations meetings was the finalized draft version of the United Nations Declaration of Indigenous Peoples Rights. The group rights issue is particularly important to indigenous peoples, who live in strong family communities. Probably the most contentious issue discussed was the right to self-determination, which brought a strong reaction from the United States delegation, which felt that it was a threat to current United States law.

It is my opinion that most of this reaction comes from misunderstanding and ignorance concerning lifestyles and governance systems of indigenous nations and peoples. Despite strong opposition on this issue, the draft declaration was completed and stands as a great achievement, representing seventeen years of work by indigenous peoples in the fields of international law.

The Subcommission on Human Rights was next on the agenda and convened throughout the month of August. It was decided that the draft declaration would be presented during the next session of the Subcommission (1994). This gives indigenous delegations time to lobby the member-states that they reside in to support the declaration as it stands without change. A highlight of the session of the Subcommission on Human Rights was the adoption of a resolution addressing the broad question of human rights in Guatemala regarding the Mayan peoples.

Unfortunately, the massacre of Yanomamis during the week of August 16 by gold prospectors in the Amazonian state of Roraima and the August 18 massacre in the Peruvian Amazon of 64 Ashaninka Indians by the Maoist guerilla group "the Shining Path" overshadowed all other events concerning indigenous peoples in 1993. The irony of these massacres occurring during the International Year illustrates how little progress has been made in the human rights of indigenous peoples since the landing of Christopher Columbus.

It has been five hundred years of genocide for the same reason: GOLD! These latest atrocities committed against indigenous peoples bring a hard twist to the realities of our times. The gold prospectors responsible for the murders of these innocent people make clear that the savagery of "civilized" peoples in quest for riches at the expense of moral law continues and is expanding with the world market.

Indigenous peoples will continue to be victims of this greed as long as we have lands and territories with natural resources, or until the values of civilization change. These tragedies only strengthen our resolve and will to survive.

There is a race between "profits now" and the survival of our grandchildren.

There is a race between common sense and the world market.

The race is in progress; this generation and the next will determine the outcome.

Who will write that epilogue?

Joagquisho (Oren Lyons)
Onondaga Nation

Regional Communiqués: The Struggle for Survival

Selected Indigenous Populations of Central and South America

CENTRAL AND SOUTH AMERICA

José Barriero

In the vast region that includes Central America, South America, and the Caribbean islands, there are today over 500 Indian nationalities, speaking hundreds of native languages, and living in terrain, climate, and under social conditions that are equally distinct. The 40 million indigenous people who live in this region include those with the earliest recorded contact with Europeans, the Tainos, who met Columbus's first voyage; and those with the latest contact, the Yanomami of the remote upper Amazon basin, who were only "discovered" in the late twentieth century.

While their cultures are diverse and often strikingly different—and continually changing—there is a unity that bonds these many nations: they share a common history. They had a distinctly non-Western philosophy and way of thought, and they are today largely dispossessed of their rights as nations of people.

Since the invasion of explorers and conquistadors such as Columbus, who subjugated much of the Caribbean; Pizzaro, who conquered the Inca Empire; and Cabral, who invaded Brazil; whole Indian nations have disappeared through warfare, cruelty, and disease. For five hundred years, Indians have endured the theft of their lands and natural resources, the enslavement of most of their people, and the domination by a new cultural and philosophical system completely alien to them. Indian beliefs were persecuted, their books destroyed, their languages repressed, and they and their children humiliated at every turn, through the introduction of racism.

Yet, today Indians are still unconquered, resisting domination, retaking ancestral lands, demanding a voice in their own affairs, and rebuilding cultures and nations. They struggle and endure despite living in countries that are among the most brutal in the world, despite the tremendous poverty of the region, and despite the enormous national and international pressure to destroy and exploit every natural region and resource. The voice of these people is being heard by more and more of the non-Indian world, and that voice is no longer heard so much for its heresies as for the answers it may offer to the problems of the modern world.

Few periods in history, certainly in the past century, have been as terrifying for a people as the repression of indigenous people in Guatemala. Of its 9 million inhabitants, over 5 million are Mayan Indians, and most of the rest of the population is of mixed blood. Between 1981 and 1983, under the "pacification" programs of the Guatemalan dictator General Efrain Rios Montt almost 1 million Mayas were forcibly displaced, many of them into "model villages" that more resembled concentration camps. Over 20,000 Indians were killed and more than 250 villages destroyed.

The use of a scorched earth policy as well as torture continued throughout the 1980s. Despite attempts to reform the government, today the military continues to operate independently and is still a force of terror to the native populations. The awarding of the Nobel Peace Prize to Rigoberta Menchú, a Mayan woman who lost most of her family to army massacres and was forced to flee to Mexico, is only a small step in recognizing the terrible plight of many native peoples in Latin America.

A different outcome, through a different set of circumstances, has brought the Miskito Indians of Nicaragua an autonomy that is largely unknown to the rest of the region. Largely isolated on the country's Atlantic coast, they were generally ignored under the repressive regime of General Anastasio Somoza Debayle. His overthrow by Sandinista rebels, who then attempted to consolidate the country, led to conflict between the Miskitos and the Sandinistas. The conflict was made more complex by the larger struggle between the Sandinistas and the United States. Fighting the Sandinistas to a standstill, the Miskitos, through strong village leadership, have now carved out a strong role in Nicaraguan politics. Working to become more self-sufficient, while maintaining their agricultural and fishing lifestyle, they recently rebuffed an attempt by Nicaragua and international interests to log their forests.

As I write this, a massacre has just occurred in Brazil, where 70 Yanomami Indians, men, women, and children, were brutally slain by gold miners who refuse to recognize Yanomami land rights. During the past twenty years the government at an ever-accelerating rate, colonized and destroyed the great Amazon rain forest, the richest, most biologically diverse region on the planet. This rush to development, which included gold mining, ranching, lumber projects, and road building, was done without any regard for native rights to the land. Like similar land rushes in the past, disease and violence devastated dozens of Indian tribes, including Waimiri and Atroari people, whose population dropped by more than two- thirds in this period. While recently lands have been set aside by the Brazilian government for the Indians of the Amazon, they are still beset by illegal trespassers, who are becoming increasingly violent. Under tremendous international pressure, President Fernando Collor de Mello set aside a natural park for the Yanomami in 1991 and began evicting the miners. His recent removal from office, however, has encouraged the Brazilian Parliament to try to do away with Indian lands altogether.

In Paraguay, only recently people were still hunting Indians like game. Less than twenty years ago, the Ayoreo and Ache people were regularly captured and sold as slaves. Relocations, such as the removal of the Toba-Maskoy people to the barren Chaco Desert, were common. Missionary organizations, which operate in most of Latin America, have largely completed the genocidal process in that country, by descending on a broken people and destroying what was left of their culture.

In Peru, the $9\frac{1}{4}$ million Indians suffer, not only from the usual expropriation of their lands by multinational corporations, exploitation as cheap labor or serfdom, denial of religious freedom, and brutality from an oppressive government, but they are also victimized by Maoist rebels, "the Shining

Path." In a violent and terrifying world, especially for Indians, "the Shining Path" is virtually unmatched for its merciless and arbitrary killing sprees. It terrorizes the Quechuas and Aymaras, only this past month massacring a village of 200, simply for the sake of causing terror. Add to that the power and violence of drug lords who preside over billions of dollars of ill-gotten gains, and one must admire and appreciate the great courage of a gentle people who survive as one of the oldest known cultures in the world.

These situations are, of course, only a small sample of the issues affecting the region. Indians in Columbia, Chile, Venezuela, and Bolivia all suffer from governments that do not respect their rights to land, or even existence. Yet vast local and regional movements, such as the Indigenous Confederation of Ecuador (CONAIE), have become major political forces in their countries.

I would close with the work that is going on, beneath the acts of violence, the destruction of the earth, and noise of Western culture. Even the devastation of Columbus and his successors, who decimated the islands of the Caribbean, could not wipe out the Indian roots of those islands. Today, many descendants of the people of the Caribbean are turning over the layers of progress, like turning over soil, and finding those roots. Nations such as the Taino and Carib are rising from the past, and indeed the work of rebuilding the earth may have just begun.

José Barriero is the editor of Ake:kon Press and the author of The Indian Chronicles.

NORTH AMERICA
Ingrid Washinawatok-El Issa

A broad look at the North American continent five hundred years ago would provide some remarkable observations about the indigenous cultures that flourished then. It was a continent that in many respects was a model of diversity. In central Mexico, were the grand city-state empires of the Aztecs, the Tarascans, and the Mayas, who built some of the largest pyramids in the world and had sophisticated sciences, technology, and agriculture. In the eastern part of what is now the United States were the large confederacies such as the Iroquois, the Creek, and the Cherokee, with matrilineal governments that were among the most democratic and egalitarian the world has ever known. Along the northwest coast lived the wealthy seafaring fishermen, who communed deeply with the spirits of animals and fish. The frozen north held Inuit people who could live and thrive under conditions that daunt modern technology. In the endless sea of buffalo that made up the Great Plains, the Sioux, Crow, and Comanche lived a free, loose life that continues to capture the imagination to this very day. Indeed, every region was remarkably different, very similar to the enormous biological diversity that existed at that time.

While it is difficult to estimate the number of Indians living on the continent in 1492, it is known that Tenochtitlan, the Aztec capital, was then among the largest cities in the world, and there was little of this continent that was not settled. The great ability of the native people to work with the environment, rather than against it, gave this continent the appearance of a vast wilderness, though most of it was managed in one way or another. Dispensing with the myth of an empty continent, an estimate of 30 million Indians in 1492 is a conservative figure.

This great continental richness, biological and cultural, was not appreciated by the European settler and conquistador. The great Indian nations were broken up and dispersed and the

131

Selected Indigenous Populations of North America

vast, managed wilderness destroyed. Yet the Indians of North America still hold to their many traditions, cultures, and religions. The continuing diversity of native people is reflected not only in their arts and religion, but also in their struggles.

In the United States, where 90 percent of the native land base has been taken over the past 250 years, one-quarter of the Indians live on over 300 reservations that are autonomous governments under American law, subject only to federal authority. While this autonomy is continually challenged and sometimes chipped slightly, it has allowed for, among other things, an explosive growth in casinos and gaming on Indian reservations, an industry that is illegal in most of the United States. This autonomy has also been seen by producers of toxic nuclear and other wastes as a way to circumvent environmental regulations and public opposition to waste dumps and storage sites. At least two reservations in the United States, those of the Mescalero Apaches and the Skull Valley Goshutes, have entered into negotiations with the federal government to become repositories for high-level nuclear waste.

These industries have been accepted by some Indian reservations largely because of the historic poverty of Indians in the United States. While the Indian nations negotiated hundreds of treaties with the United States government, all were broken, and the former owners of the land were robbed of everything. Even today, Indians in the United States suffer from the highest unemployment rate, the highest rate of poverty, the highest infant mortality rate, the highest rate of teenage suicide, the highest rate of diabetes, the greatest incidence of malnutrition, the highest susceptibility to disease, the lowest per capita income, the shortest life expectancy, the poorest education, the highest federal imprisonment rate, and the lowest standard of living.

Most tribes have not renounced their strong ethic of living in harmony with the environment in return for Western-style development. Most Indian lands are still well cared for, and many support animal and plant species that have disappeared from the rest of the United States. However, the traditions of

American Indians are under constant threat of erosion from a continuing lack of religious freedom and the destruction of sacred sites, the continuing racism that pervades American society, or the tremendous dominance and influence of American cultural institutions, such as television. Urban Indians now number more than reservation Indians, and their efforts to pass on their traditions to their children in the environment of the American city face overwhelming odds.

Virtually every Indian community has a struggle of some kind or another, yet some of the most pressing issues involve defending the earth. In the 1980s thousands of Navajos were relocated, and are still being removed, from their lands in the southwestern United States, ostensibly at the demand of the neighboring Hopi tribe, but in reality to pave the way for energy development. In the state of Nevada there is a continuing battle between the Western Shoshone and the Bureau of Land Management, an agency with a poor reputation for environmental protection, in which the bureau is trying to seize Indian lands in defiance of a hundred-year-old treaty. The Lummi of the northwest coast are trying to stop the clearcutting of forests next to their lands by an insurance company, an act that would destroy salmon runs and disturb the nesting sites of a host of endangered bird species. In the East, the Mohawks of Akwesasne have been fighting smelters and other heavy industries that have virtually destroyed the St. Lawrence Seaway and surrounding regions with toxic wastes and heavy metals, poisoning the reservation's water supply and lands.

While it might at first glance appear that the autonomous nature of Indian reservations might be an aid in combatting struggles such as these, the nature of Indian governments often only exacerbates problems. With the notable exception of the Iroquois Confederacy, almost all Indian governments in the United States were set up by the United States government in the 1930s, without taking into account the traditional Indian process of governance. Many of these new governments were simply puppets of the United States, and its notoriously corrupt Bureau of Indian Affairs, and became agents for further defrauding Indian people. In Alaska, the indigenous communities were turned into corporations, with the native people becoming shareholders by legislation in the 1970s. This arrangement has led to a host of new problems. Leadership conflicts continue in many areas, often dividing Indian reservations into opposing factions. While the Indians of the United States may possess a certain amount of sovereignty that Indians in other countries still strive to achieve, American Indian governments are often still beholden to the United States.

In Mexico, the Indian people hold no such rights. With by far and away the largest population of Indians in the Western Hemisphere today, over 20 million as compared to only 2 million in the United States and 1 million in Canada, Indians are the lowest and poorest class in a Mexican society that is still highly stratified. Over 6 million Mexican Indians still speak one of the 220 Indian languages, more languages than in the United States and Canada combined. Most of the Indians in Mexico, however, have lost their native religions and are largely Roman Catholic.

Unlike Dutch and British policies, which largely practiced the removal of Indians and the segregation of peoples, Spanish doctrine preached the incorporation of Mexican Indians into Spanish society. In practice, Indians became serfs under the *encommienda* system, and the cruelty of Spanish rule helped put Indians at the forefront of the Mexican revolutions that would overthrow European dominance.

Today, Indian governments are not recognized by the Mexican government, and Indians do not have reservations. Their lands, like most lands in Mexico, are the common property of all Mexicans, and arbitrary expropriations, relocations, and destructive development are quite common. Unlike Native American groups in the United States, Mexican Indians have directed much of their political activity toward mainstream politics. Since its inception, Mexico has had three Indian presidents, and Indian votes continue to be crucial in the electoral process. Mexico has also incorporated its Indian heritage into its mainstream culture to a far greater extent than have the United States or Canada.

Yet violations of Indian rights are quite common throughout the country. In the Yucatán and Chiapas rain forest, Mayan Indians are subject to increasing threats from massive forestry projects and encroachment by poor pioneers. Lack of title to their lands means northern Mexican Indians, such as the Yaqui, Apache, and Tohono O'odham, have been forced off their lands by Mexican officials who deed their ancestral lands to settlers and speculators. The poverty of Mexican Indians is widespread and much worse than just about anything experienced in the United States.

The largest threat to Mexican Indians, however, comes from the North American Free Trade Agreement (NAFTA) and other such initiatives. Most Indians live at a subsistence level by cultivating corn or maize, the ancient grain developed in Mexico. Free trade agreements would likely unleash a wave of American corn, grown through modern agribusiness techniques and force Mexican growers to do the same—probably forcing most of the Indian farmers off their land and into the overpopulated Mexican cities.

Modern free trade also poses a serious threat to Canadian Indians and Inuit peoples, who continue to hold title to the largest natural land areas in the Western Hemisphere. The British, French, and Canadian governments signed few treaties with the indigenous people of Canada. The isolation and harsh climate of the Canadian north have delayed the exploitation of the vast wilderness, but modern technology and the dwindling supply of natural resources are likely to make Canada the new battleground for native rights in the near future.

The Canadian government, like the American, bases its claims to land within its boundaries on a legal philosophy known as the "Doctrine of Discovery." Under this doctrine, the "discovery" of Canada by a European explorer, who then claimed all of it for his Crown, granted to Canada all title to the land. Despite having lived on this continent for thousands of years, if Indians wish to have any rights to their own lands, they must negotiate with Canada for them. The obvious fiction of such a legal doctrine means that in reality many of the Indians have still not given up title to their land, since they neither negotiated nor have signed treaties. Canada has embarked on a pursuit of new treaties and agreements with Indians in an attempt to forestall future challenges to the "Doctrine of Discovery." Among these new treaties is the creation of the territory of Nunavit, carved out from the Northwest Territories. While providing the Inuit with some of their original land base and a significant monetary compensation, the Inuit still cede control over mineral and other development in the region and may be unable to stop the negative environmental and cultural consequences that such projects bring.

Canada needs clear title to Indian lands and resources because it has embarked on projects designed to exploit what is the largest pristine wilderness in the hemisphere. From the lands of the Algonquin Indians in Quebec to those of the Lil'wat in British Columbia, native forests are being clear-cut at a rate much higher even than in the Amazon. Canada, the largest diverter of rivers on the continent, is planning some of the most massive hydroelectric and water transfer projects in the world. Virtually no river in its territories is safe. One project alone, the James Bay II project in northern Quebec, is the largest industrial project in the history of North America; when completed, it would badly degrade a pristine area the size of France. The Cree and Inuit of Quebec have fought this project to a standstill; however, other Indians are doing less well. The Piegan attempts to stop the Old Man river dam in Alberta and Inuit attempts to fight the Lower Churchill Falls hydroelectric project in Labrador and Moise River diversion in Quebec together with a widely based movement to stop massive water transfers from northern rivers to the southwest and western United States, are all ongoing.

Indian governments in Canada are largely modeled after those in the United States, with many of the same problems. However, they have far less power than their American counterparts, and there are frequent attempts by the Canadian government to reduce their influence further. Canada does provide native people with more comprehensive health, educational, and employment benefits than Mexico, where these are nonexistent, or the United States, where they are woefully mismanaged. In addition, a large portion of the Indian and Inuit population is still very traditional, maintaining ancient lifestyles, language, and religion and becoming more active in seeking out their rightful place in Canadian society.

The Indians of North America face many threats, including the inexorable homogenizing effect of modern culture that is transforming and changing native cultures and sometimes extinguishing them. Yet the great wilderness areas that continue to exist are largely in native hands, and native concepts and philosophies regarding how humans should interact with the rest of the world are finding more and more acceptance in the modern world. This is a tribute to the native people of this hemisphere, who have survived many worlds, including the modern one, and may yet survive to see yet another.

Ingrid Washinawatok-El Issa (Menominee) is the co-chair of the Indigenous Women's Network, and is a grant-making administrator for the Fund for the Four Directions.

THE PACIFIC RIM
Glen Alcalay

The aquatic continent of the Pacific Ocean usually evokes sensuous images of Gauguin's Tahitians and frivolous South Pacific islanders living carefree lives of ecstasy in a veritable Garden of Eden.

In sharp contrast to the idyllic stereotypes perpetuated by a Western world hungry for escapist illusions, the contemporary Pacific reflects the "business end" of centuries of colonialism and militarism by metropolitan powers bent on furthering their hegemonic claims in every island "paradise."

The indigenous struggle taking place in the French-held and nickel-rich island of New Caledonia represents the current face of Pacific colonialism. Since 1853 the indigenous Melanesian Kanak people have endured a steady influx of militant French *caldoche* immigrants. Having been marginalized to the least habitable portions of the island chain, the Kanaks are awaiting a 1998 referendum (based on the "Matignon Accords") to determine their future status.

Fiji, once described by the Pope as a "model for multiethnic society," gave the Pacific its first military coup d'etat in 1987 after deposing the progressive and antinuclear Labour Government of Timoci Bavandra. Now headed by the coup-maker, General Rabuka, post-coup Fiji simmers in a tense state of racial anxiety between the indigenous Melanesians and the Indo-Fijians.

In the not-so-pacific-Pacific, Native Hawaiians have mounted an increasingly successful campaign for Hawaiian sovereignty and the return of prime native lands. Concomitant with the push for Hawaiian sovereignty is a renewal of Hawaiian culture, including the Hawaiian language and the hula.

The Marshall Islands were targeted by the Pentagon as the nuclear test laboratories for the United States' postwar development of the atomic and hydrogen bombs. After some sixty-six nuclear weapons explosions and the disappearance of entire islands coupled with the sociological dislocation of several island communities, thousands of downwind Marshallese continue to suffer the wrath of the "peaceful atom" amidst contaminated islands and lagoons decades after the last test at Bikini and Enewetak. In a recently released document from a 1956 meeting of the Atomic Energy Commission, it was boldly stated that

> Utirik is safe to live on but is by far the most contaminated place in the world, and it will be very interesting to go back and get good environmental data. Now data of this type has never been available. While it is true that these people do not live the way westerners do, civilized people [sic], it is nevertheless also true that these people are more like us than the mice.

In Tahiti, the icon of Eden itself, the Maohi people also struggle against the *force de frappé*, or the so-called French "nuclear deterrent" policy of developing these destructive weapons 7,000 miles from Paris. Led by independence leader and Mayor of Faa'a (Tahiti's second largest city) Oscar Temaru, the Tahitian sovereignty movement is gaining momentum in the new world order.

Recently, the entire Pacific community was galvanized by the United States's decision to destroy chemical and nerve gas weapons brought from Okinawa and Germany at an incineration plant on Johnston Atoll. Lying 700 miles southwest of Hawaii—and under United States control since 1858—Johnston is the site of the $150 million JACADS (Johnston Atoll Chemical Agent Disposal System) incinerator, which could release carcinogenic material into the atmosphere and onto the sea surface microlayer. It is believed that Johnston will also play a role in a Pentagon scheme to train soldiers in the handling and use of chemical weapons in war.

Guam, captured along with the Philippines and Puerto Rico after the Spanish-American War in 1898, is the jewel of all the Micronesian islands. After it was claimed by Magellan in 1521,

Spanish troops waged a war of extermination against the indigenous Chamorro people. With the help of introduced diseases like smallpox and syphilis, the Chamorros were reduced from an original population of 80,000 in 1668 to fewer than 5,000 in 1741. By 1783 their numbers had been further reduced to a mere 1,500.

The Pentagon stations 21,000 United States military personnel, spends $750 million a year, and controls one-third of Guam's 216 square miles. The current population of 130,000—comprised of mixed blood Chamorros, Japanese, Filipinos, Chinese, and Koreans—has been Westernized and disrupted by this overbearing presence. Home to the Pacific Strategic Air Command (which proved useful for B-52 sorties during the Vietnam War), Guam is also the central command for the Communications Area Master Station for all western Pacific United States naval forces.

The indigenous Chamorros have been protesting to the United Nations and Congress for years about environmental contamination from the military bases, and they have also intensified their campaign to retake land seized by the United States for military purposes.

Heading the list of Pacific island nations currently embroiled in civil strife is Papua New Guinea, which is faced with a secessionist struggle on the copper-rich island of Bougainville. In the neocolonial era, the PNG regime in Port Moresby has taken a hard line to suppress the insurgent Bougainville Revolutionary Army uprising.

In the tiny Micronesian island nation of Bel—500 miles from the Philippines—the United States has long coveted military and counterinsurgency bases. Having created the world's first antinuclear constitution in 1979, Belauans became an international cause célèbre. Following the assassination of Belau's first elected president, Haruo Remeliik, and the apparent suicide of its second president, Lazarus Salii, twelve referenda in as many years (fueled by extreme economic and political pressures from Washington) have torn the troubled nation in myriad ways. Thus far the Belauans have firmly rejected an expanded United States military presence.

Since 1975, says Timorese resistance leader Xanana Gusmao, the East Timorese people have "lived under an injustice" based on a betrayal of universal principles. According to Xanana:

> Some people talk about the difference of principle between what has happened in Kuwait and East Timor. . . . Ironically, those who defend this indefensible thesis admit that the way East Timor was annexed does not conform with the norms set for nonself-governing territories, implicitly recognizing that the invasion and military occupation [by the Indonesian army] of East Timor is illegal. As regards the violation of borders, the use of force and so on, Kuwait is a carbon copy of what happened in East Timor.

Since he spoke these words in 1991, Xanana was captured by the Indonesian army and faces a treason charge with a possible death sentence.

In Polynesia, moves toward democracy have gained momentum. Western Samoa in April 1991 held its first general election under universal suffrage since gaining independence from New Zealand in 1962. In the neighboring conservative kingdom of Tonga, the struggle for greater accountability and open government achieved a remarkable moral victory in February 1991, led by the fearless opposition leader Akilisi Pohiva.

Since 1975, the burgeoning Nuclear Free and Independent Pacific (NFIP) movement has led a grassroots campaign to decolonize and demilitarize the Pacific region. In recent years, the NFIP has made important links with indigenous struggles in Turtle Island and Latin America. The NFIP movement has helped to put fire under the flaccid South Pacific Forum—comprised of the heads of government from Pacific island states—and has succeeded in conducting a massive public education campaign concerning the destabilizing effects of colonization and militarism in the region.

The speeches of indigenous leaders to the United Nations bear witness to many of these Pacific struggles. The many poignant voices heard at the United Nations speak both to our intellect and our hearts. These voices of resistance derive from the souls of those who have been on the front lines combatting imperialism, racism, and the brutality of militarism. It is an honor to introduce these courageous fighters for social justice and world peace.

Glenn Alcalay is Assistant Professor of Anthropology at Dowling College, Long Island, New York, and has been active in the Pacific indigenous struggle for the past eighteen years. He also works with the World Uranium Hearing, a global antinuclear organization based in New York City.

Selected Indigenous Populations of Africa

AFRICA AND EURASIA
Alexander Ewen

At the end of 1993, it was estimated that indigenous people still maintained control over 12 percent of the land on this planet. Almost all of this area is still in a natural state—and almost all of it, along with the indigenous people themselves, is now threatened by development. Vast regions of wilderness, including the largest remaining forest in the world, Siberia's evergreen forest, have been targeted for exploitation since the fall of the Communist Bloc. Africa, only one hundred years ago an "unknown" primordial landscape, may lose its great rain forests by the turn of the next century.

With the possible exception of the European subcontinent, where indigenous people have been largely decimated or assimilated, Eurasia and Africa are not known for an abundance of democratic governments. Of the approximately one hundred armed conflicts underway in 1993, seventy involved state aggression against minority communities. Southeast Asia, the Middle East, central and northern Africa, all wracked by war and famine, have become bloody battlegrounds in which indigenous communities are simply pawns in global power politics.

The 200 million indigenous people of these regions face additional threats from the changing economic order, which is becoming more global—and more antidemocratic—every day. Native peoples are rapidly being forced into the consumer economy and their resources auctioned in the global marketplace. These new economic trends are directly tied to continuing aggression against indigenous people and are making conditions worse, not better, for the vast majority of them.

Africa

In Africa, the term indigenous peoples is generally used only for nomadic or pastoral tribal groups, largely restricted by the "forward-looking" African governments, who wish to bury their precolonial heritage and join the "modern world." Africa is home to approximately 30 million nomadic peoples and millions more pastoralists such as the Masai. However, in most African countries, between 75 and 90 percent of the people are farmers who live a life similar to that of peoples who are termed "indigenous" on the other continents.

Attempting to conform to international standards of commerce, African governments have been driving nomadic tribal peoples off their lands with brutal determination. An example is Tanzania, where some 30,000 Baribaigs whose grazing lands are being expropriated for commercial wheat production. Families are forced off their lands by government authorities at gunpoint and without compensation. Tanzania refuses to recognize Baribaig ownership of their lands, considering them to be "primitive people." In this case, the driving force behind the removal of the Baribaigs comes, not from multinational agribusiness, but from "aid" schemes by developed countries such as Canada. To combat chronic hunger, these countries generously support the commercial production of crops such as wheat while presumably looking the other way as land for these development projects is unethically obtained.

The 200,000 Pygmies in central Africa are only one of 450 forest peoples threatened by increasing pressure to log the great tropical rain forests of the Zaire Basin. The African continent has the highest deforestation rate in the world: approximately 16 percent of its forests were destroyed between 1980 and 1990. The West African rain forest has already disappeared in countries such as Ghana and the Ivory Coast and is now only 40 percent of its original size. The enormous central African rain forest is the size of Western Europe and extends over more than seven countries, including the Congo, Zaire, and Gabon. It has recently become the target not only of large-scale logging by German, French, and Belgian companies, but also gold mining, commercial charcoal production, and poaching.

Attempts to preserve Africa's unique wildlife from extinction have often come at the expense of the African indigenous peoples. Indigenous peoples' lands are in many cases the last refuge of some of the most endangered African animals and therefore ideal choices for parks and game preserves. In Botswana, for example, the government has long attempted to force the G/wi from the Central Kalahari Game Preserve, though thus far without success.

Global and regional political squabbles have swept up numerous African indigenous peoples, with almost uniformly disastrous results for those peoples. European attempts to retain control of their former colonies have led to bitter rivalries that have engulfed African countries. In Angola, the bitter and bloody conflict against Portugal left 100,000 Angolans dead and 750,000 refugees. Angola's "victory" left the weak country compromised by bitter ethnic rivalries that would soon be exploited by the United States, the Soviet Union, China, Cuba, and of course, Portugal.

Soviet and American rivalry resulted in the arming of tribal peoples in Ethiopia and Somalia, leading directly to civil war and catastrophic famines. South Africa's policy of arming some of the Bushmen in Namibia has involved the Bushmen, to their regret, in Africa's longest civil war.

If these trends continue, the indigenous peoples and their unique knowledge and lifestyles may be lost forever. Plant-based medicines of the forest-dwelling Kpelle of Liberia, together with the genetic information represented in the wide variety of distinct crops that they grow, may be able to aid the world if the world can learn to appreciate the contributions of indigenous peoples. The Mbuti of Zaire, as well as the Bira, Ndaka, and Mbo, guard some of the world's rarest mammals, such as the lowland gorilla, the pygmy chimpanzee, and the okapi, all the while subsisting off the rain forest they share with these rare animals. This ability to live with nature without degrading the environment may be the most precious knowledge available to modern man. Yet it has been overlooked until it is almost too late.

Eurasia

The indigenous people of Eurasia face many of the same problems found in Africa, and one more, atomic weapons testing. The Soviet Union, China, and India conduct tests within their boundaries and on the lands of indigenous peoples. The Chinese bomb the Uygur nation, the Russians the Kombi, Yakut, and Nenet, and Indians in Rajasthan. France and Britain, being democracies, test their bombs in the Pacific Ocean on Pacific islanders such as the Australian Aborigines or Tuamotu islanders.

Not surprisingly, the three Asian nuclear powers are also the last remaining empires, in the traditional sense of the word, in the world. Between them they have subjugated hundreds of different groups, most of them indigenous peoples. Although crumbling, the Russian Federation is still geographically the largest sovereign entity in the world, home to some of the most pristine and isolated land areas and to some of the most isolated indigenous peoples. With the need to enter the world market rapidly as a capitalist country—and raise hard cash—many of these inaccessible areas, such as the Chukshis Peninsula or Russian Saamiland, can be expected to be opened to development through either joint ventures or simply by the selling off of the vast Russian natural wealth. The Soviet Union's nonexistent environmental laws have also made some areas in the former bloc among the most polluted in the world. Contamination from toxic chemicals, metal smelting, and nuclear wastes have left hundreds of regions almost uninhabitable. Diversions of rivers have caused extensive loss of wildlife. The effects of the Chernobyl nuclear disaster are still being felt by the Saami of Norway, Finland, and northern Russia. The most obvious effect is the decimation of their reindeer herds by nuclear fallout.

The indigenous population of South Asia is approximately 51 million, the largest number found in any single region. Many of them live in India, a land of hundreds of different tribal and ethnic groups. India is well known for human rights abuses against its indigenous people, including torture and execution of the Naga people of the northern Manipur district and the Bodo of Assam. In western India a struggle is being waged to save the Narmada valley from the Sardar Sarovar and Narmada Sagar hydroelectric projects. The Sardar Sarovar project alone would flood out 130,000 of Gond, Tadavi, and Baiga tribal peoples. Neighboring Bangladesh continues its undeclared war against indigenous peoples in the Chittagong Hill Tracts. Over 114,000 soldiers stationed in the region regularly commit atrocities against the Jumma villagers, many of whom have fled to India as refugees.

The Chinese forty-year occupation of Tibet has become increasingly genocidal. Policies are being carried out against Tibetans to ensure that Tibet will always remain in the Chinese empire. Demolition of Tibetan cities, the banning of Tibetan culture, and the importation of millions of Chinese settlers are rapidly leading to the disappearance of one of the oldest and most venerated cultures in the world.

In Southeast Asia, countries such as Indonesia are among the most brutal in the world, and its indigenous peoples, such as the Timorese, have undergone a savagery at the hands of the Indonesian government that has rarely been witnessed in human history. Thailand is planning to relocate up to 4 million Hmong, Karen, and other indigenous people to make way for eucalyptus plantations. In Burma, the government has waged a forty-year war against the Arakan, Karen, Chin, and other indigenous peoples of that land. Indigenous peoples in these countries, such as the Kensue, are facing extinction as a consequence of intensive deforestation, logging, and brutal military attacks.

These acts against usually unarmed and peaceful indigenous peoples are repeated over and over again in Africa and Eurasia. The denial of indigenous rights by all the nation-states of the globe must be seen as quiet assent to the continuing genocide of the world's natural people. The United Nations' lack of active support for indigenous peoples' rights is understandable when viewed as part of the continuing struggle by

Ostia

Saami

Penga

Madia Gond

Chakma

Selected Indigenous Populations of Eurasia

Koryak

Chukchis

Gilyaks

Ainu

Wawa Taw-il

ayak

Papua

Maohi

Kanak

Torres Strait Islanders

nation-states to defend their arbitrary boundaries. No matter how divided and at odds they may be toward each other, the nation-states of the world represented at the United Nations have a common agenda: to consolidate and expand their political and economic power. The indigenous people living within their boundaries are viewed as an obstacle—even as a threat to the continued existence of the nation-state. The common denominator in government wars against these helpless and peaceful peoples is the land. Today, the land must serve the greater economic needs of the nation-state as a whole, and indigenous people are holding everything up. In the end, the indigenous people serve as the last barrier to the conquest of the world by "civilization," and a group more courageous than they simply does not exist on this planet.

Alexander Ewen (Purepecha) is the director of the Solidarity Foundation, a research foundation devoted to native issues and a member of the Native American Council of New York City.

Appendices

Appendix A

STATEMENT OF INDIGENOUS NATIONS,
PEOPLES, AND ORGANIZATIONS

Appendix B

UNITED NATIONS DRAFT DECLARATION
OF INDIGENOUS PEOPLES RIGHTS

Appendix

APPENDIX A
Statement of Indigenous Nations, Peoples, and Organizations

Gucumatz, Condor, Father Sun, Eagle, Anahuac, Mother Earth.

INVOKING the spirits of our ancestors and acting in our tradition of resistance in the defense of Mother Earth, asserting our fundamental and historical rights,

ASSERTING all the millions of brothers and sisters who have sacrificed their lives in defense of our millennial culture, In the name of the more than 300 million indigenous people which inhabit the Earth, and the efforts over the years of work by indigenous peoples and NGO's, we, the members of the INDIGENOUS NATIONS AND ORGANIZATIONS, gathered in New York City, from the 8th to the 10th of December of 1992,

WE CONSIDER:

I. That all indigenous peoples have the right to self-determination as expounded in the principles of the Universal Declaration of the Rights of Indigenous Peoples. Accordingly, indigenous peoples have the right to determine all matters relating to our political, economic, social, spiritual and cultural affairs. We call for the immediate adoption of the above declaration.

II. The struggle for our territorial rights is common to all indigenous nations and peoples, and this right is persistently denied by governments and dominant societies.

III. Economic development practices of Nation States are

destroying the natural resources which have been protected within indigenous territories. As a consequence, the survival of all species is threatened.

IV. The indigenous peoples' contribution to the social, intellectual and cultural diversity of the world, particularly to the ecology and harmony of Mother Earth must be valued and supported by Nation States and international agencies.

V. The human rights of indigenous peoples to our culture, identity, religions and languages are inalienable. These rights continue to be sacrificed in the programs, policies and budgets of the Nation States and international agencies.

VI. While democracy is heralded by dominant societies, what this means to indigenous peoples is repression, genocide and misery in the Americas and in the rest of the world. As an example, [in] the process by which the dialogue for peace is taking place in Central and South America, there is no direct participation by indigenous organizations and nations in spite of the fact that indigenous peoples are directly affected by the conditions of the wars.

VII. The survival of indigenous sovereign governments continues in spite of the oppressive actions and programs of the Nation States and the dominant society.

VIII. Governments continue to desecrate and appropriate religious and sacred places and objects, depriving indigenous nations around the world of their basic spiritual ways of life.

THEREFORE: The International Year of the World's Indigenous People, 1993, must not be merely celebrations or paternalistic declarations, but rather, the resolution of the above requires that the United Nations and its member-states take the following actions:

1. Recognize indigenous rights to indigenous territories, including the recovery and demarcation of such territories.

2. Recognize, honor, and document under international law all treaties, compacts, accords and other formal agreements concluded with indigenous peoples of the world. Additionally the Study on Indigenous Treaties delegated to the Human Rights Commission must be given priority attention by the United Nations and its member-states.

3. Recognize and honor indigenous forms of government when such governments are practiced according to traditional laws and customs.

4. Promote and strengthen indigenous intellectual and cultural property rights under International Law and principles. Additionally, the study on intellectual and cultural property rights undertaken by the United Nations Commission on Human Rights should be given priority.

5. Consult with indigenous organizations and nations regarding the ratification of Covenant 169 of the International Labor Organization.

6. Provide legal assistance and technical training to the indigenous organizations and nations.

7. Promote at the national and international levels the reform of laws and policies such that they recognize the sovereign rights of the indigenous peoples.

8. Promote and strengthen indigenous education, culture, art, religion, philosophies, literature and sciences of indigenous nations.

9. Return historic places and sacred sites and objects to the indigenous nations to whom they belong.

10. Demonstrate sincere commitment to the new partnership with indigneous peoples by making adequate financial resources available to implement actions presented herein. Furthermore, make significant donations to the Voluntary Fund so that future projects be realized, and assure that the indigenous peoples have direct input into the management of said fund.

11. That the United Nations Secretary General and its specialized agencies, commissions and programs convene special consultations with indigenous peoples of the world at the most local level practical.

12. That the Secretary General of the United Nations create immediately a specific indigenous program to be administered and executed with direct participation of indigenous organizations.

Written in the City of New York, 9 December, 1992

APPENDIX B
United Nations Draft Declaration of Indigenous Peoples Rights

Annex I

DRAFT DECLARATION AS AGREED UPON
BY THE MEMBERS OF THE WORKING
GROUP AT ITS ELEVENTH SESSION

Affirming that indigenous peoples are equal in dignity and rights to all other peoples, while recognizing the right of all peoples to be different, to consider themselves different, and to be respected as such,

Affirming also that all peoples contribute to the diversity and richness of civilizations and cultures, which constitute the common heritage of humankind,

Affirming further that all doctrines, policies and practices based on or advocating superiority of peoples or individuals on the basis of national origin, racial, religious, ethnic or cultural differences are racist, scientifically false, legally invalid, morally condemnable and socially unjust,

Reaffirming also that indigenous peoples, in the exercise of their rights, should be free from discrimination of any kind,

Concerned that indigenous peoples have been deprived of their human rights and fundamental freedoms, resulting, *inter alia*, in their colonization and dispossession of their lands, territories and resources, thus preventing them from exercising, in particular, their right to development in accordance with their own needs and interests,

Recognizing the urgent need to respect and promote the inherent rights and characteristics of indigenous peoples, especially their rights to their lands, territories and resources, which derive from their political, economic and social structures and from their cultures, spiritual traditions, histories and philosophies,

Welcoming the fact that indigenous peoples are organizing themselves for political, economic, social and cultural enhancement and in order to bring an end to all forms of discrimination and oppression wherever they occur,

Convinced that control by indigenous peoples over developments affecting them and their lands, territories and resources will enable them to maintain and strengthen their institutions, cultures and traditions, and to promote their development in accordance with their aspirations and needs,

Recognizing also that respect for indigenous knowledge, cultures and traditional practices contributes to sustainable and equitable development and proper management of the environment,

Emphasizing the need for demilitarization of the lands and territories of indigenous peoples, which will contribute to peace, economic and social progress and development, understanding and friendly relations among nations and peoples of the world,

Recognizing in particular the right of indigenous families and communities to retain shared responsibility for the upbringing, training, education and well-being of their children,

Recognizing also that indigenous peoples have the right freely to determine their relationships with States in a spirit of coexistence, mutual benefit and full respect,

Considering that treaties, agreements and other arrangements between States and indigenous peoples are properly matters of international concern and responsibility,

Acknowledging that the Charter of the United Nations, the International Covenant on Economic, Social and Cultural Rights and the International Covenant on Civil and Political Rights affirm the fundamental importance of the right of self-determination of all peoples, by virtue of which they freely determine their political status and freely pursue their economic, social and cultural development,

Bearing in mind that nothing in this Declaration may be used to deny any peoples their right of self-determination,

Encouraging States to comply with and effectively implement all international instruments, in particular those related to human rights, as they apply to indigenous peoples, in consultation and cooperation with the peoples concerned,

Emphasizing that the United Nations has an important and continuing role to play in promoting and protecting the rights of indigenous peoples,

Believing that this Declaration is a further important step forward for the recognition, promotion and protection of the rights and freedoms of indigenous peoples and in the development of relevant activities of the United Nations system in this field,

Solemnly proclaims the following United Nations Declaration on the Rights of Indigenous Peoples:

PART I

Article 1

Indigenous peoples have the right to the full and effective enjoyment of all human rights and fundamental freedoms recognized in the Charter of the United Nations, the Universal Declaration of Human Rights and international human rights law.

Article 2

Indigenous individuals and peoples are free and equal to all other individuals and peoples in dignity and rights, and have the right to be free from any kind of adverse discrimination, in particular that based on their indigenous origin or identity.

Article 3

Indigenous peoples have the right of self-determination. By virtue of that right they freely determine their political status and freely pursue their economic, social and cultural development.

Article 4

Indigenous peoples have the right to maintain and strengthen their distinct political, economic, social and cultural characteristics, as well as their legal systems, while retaining their rights to participate fully, if they so choose, in the political, economic, social and cultural life of the State.

Article 5

Every indigenous individual has the right to a nationality.

PART II

Article 6

Indigenous peoples have the collective right to live in freedom, peace and security as distinct peoples and to full guarantees against genocide or any other act of violence, including the removal of indigenous children from their families and communities under any pretext.

In addition, they have the individual rights to life, physical and mental integrity, liberty and security of person.

Article 7

Indigenous peoples have the collective and individual right not to be subjected to ethnocide and cultural genocide, including prevention of and redress for:

(a) Any action which has the aim or effect of depriving them of their integrity as distinct peoples, or of their cultural values or ethnic identities;

(b) Any action which has the aim or effect of dispossessing them of their lands, territories or resources;

(c) Any form of population transfer which has the aim or effect of violating or undermining any of their rights;

(d) Any form of assimilation or integration by other cultures or ways of life imposed on them by legislative, administrative or other measures;

(e) Any form of propaganda directed against them.

Article 8

Indigenous peoples have the collective and individual right to maintain and develop their distinct identities and characteristics, including the right to identify themselves as indigenous and to be recognized as such.

Article 9

Indigenous peoples and individuals have the right to belong to an indigenous community or nation, in accordance with the traditions and customs of the community or nation concerned. No disadvantage of any kind may arise from the exercise of such a right.

Article 10

Indigenous peoples shall not be forcibly removed from their lands or territories. No relocation shall take place without the free and informed consent of the indigenous peoples concerned and after agreement on just and fair compensation and, where possible, with the option of return.

Article 11

Indigenous peoples have the right to special protection and security in periods of armed conflict.

States shall observe international standards, in particular the Fourth Geneva Convention of 1949, for the protection of civilian populations in circumstances of emergency and armed conflict, and shall not:

(a) Recruit indigenous individuals against their will into the armed forces and, in particular, for use against other indigenous peoples;

(b) Recruit indigenous children into the armed forces under any circumstances;

(c) Force indigenous individuals to abandon their land, territories or means of subsistence, or relocate them in special centres for military purposes;

(d) Force indigenous individuals to work for military purposes under any discriminatory conditions.

PART III

Article 12

Indigenous peoples have the right to practice and revitalize their cultural traditions and customs. This includes the right to maintain, protect and develop the past, present and future manifestations of their cultures, such as archaeological and historical sites, artifacts, designs, ceremonies, technologies and visual and performing arts and literature, as well as the right to the restitution of cultural, intellectual, religious and spiritual property taken without their free and informed consent or in violation of their laws, traditions and customs.

Article 13

Indigenous peoples have the right to manifest, practice, develop and teach their spiritual and religious traditions, customs and ceremonies; the right to maintain, protect, and have access in privacy to their religious and cultural sites; the right to the use and control of ceremonial objects; and the right to the repatriation of human remains.

States shall take effective measures, in conjunction with the indigenous peoples concerned, to ensure that indigenous sacred places, including burial sites, be preserved, respected and protected.

Article 14

Indigenous peoples have the right to revitalize, use, develop and transmit to future generations their histories, languages, oral traditions, philosophies, writing systems and literatures, and to designate and retain their own names for communities, places and persons.

States shall take effective measures, whenever any rights of indigenous peoples may be threatened, to ensure this right is protected and also to ensure that they can understand and be understood in political, legal and administrative proceedings, where necessary through the provision of interpretation or by other appropriate means.

PART IV

Article 15

Indigenous children have the right to all levels and forms of education of the State. All indigenous peoples also have this right and the right to establish and control their educational systems and institutions providing education in their own languages, in a manner appropriate to their cultural methods of teaching and learning.

Indigenous children living outside their communities have the right to be provided access to education in their own culture and language.

States shall take effective measures to provide appropriate resources for these purposes.

Article 16

Indigenous peoples have the right to have the dignity and diversity of their cultures, traditions, histories and aspirations appropriately reflected in all forms of education and public information.

States shall take effective measures, in consultation with the indigenous peoples concerned, to eliminate prejudice and discrimination and to promote tolerance, understanding and good relations among indigenous peoples and all segments of society.

Article 17

Indigenous peoples have the right to establish their own media in their own languages. They also have the right to equal access to all forms of non-indigenous media.

States shall take effective measures to ensure that State-owned media duly reflect indigenous cultural diversity.

Article 18

Indigenous peoples have the right to enjoy fully all rights established under international labor law and national labor legislation.

Indigenous individuals have the right not to be subjected to any discriminatory conditions of labor, employment or salary.

PART V

Article 19

Indigenous peoples have the right to participate fully, if they so choose, at all levels of decision-making in matters which may affect their rights, lives and destinies through representatives chosen by themselves in accordance with their own procedures, as well as to maintain and develop their own indigenous decision-making institutions.

Article 20

Indigenous peoples have the right to participate fully, if they so choose, through procedures determined by them, in devising legislative or administrative measures that may affect them.

States shall obtain the free and informed consent of the peoples concerned before adopting and implementing such measures.

Article 21

Indigenous peoples have the right to maintain and develop their political, economic and social systems, to be secure in the enjoyment of their own means of subsistence and development, and to engage freely in all their traditional and other economic activities. Indigenous peoples who have been deprived of their means of subsistence and development are entitled to just and fair compensation.

Article 22

Indigenous peoples have the right to special measures for the immediate, effective and continuing improvement of their economic and social conditions, including in the areas of employment, vocational training and retraining, housing, sanitation, health and social security.

Particular attention shall be paid to the rights and special needs of indigenous elders, women, youth, children and disabled persons.

Article 23

Indigenous peoples have the right to determine and develop priorities and strategies for exercising their right to development. In particular, indigenous peoples have the right to determine and develop all health, housing and other economic and social programmes affecting them and, as far as possible, to administer such programmes through their own institutions.

Article 24

Indigenous peoples have the right to their traditional medicines and health practices, including the right to the protection of vital medicinal plants, animals and minerals.

They also have the right to access, without any discrimination, to all medical institutions, health services and medical care.

PART VI

Article 25

Indigenous peoples have the right to maintain and strengthen their distinctive spiritual and material relationship with the lands, territories, waters and coastal seas and other resources which they have traditionally owned or otherwise occupied or used, and to uphold their responsibilities to future generations in this regard.

Article 26

Indigenous peoples have the right to own, develop, control and use the lands and territories, including the total environment of the lands, air, waters, coastal seas, sea-ice, flora and fauna and other resources which they have traditionally owned or otherwise occupied or used. This includes the right to the full recognition of their laws, traditions and customs, land-tenure systems and institutions for the development and management of resources, and the right to effective measures by States to prevent any interference with, alienation of or encroachment upon these rights.

Article 27

Indigenous peoples have the right to the restitution of the lands, territories and resources which they have traditionally owned or otherwise occupied or used, and which have been confiscated, occupied, used or damaged without their free and informed consent. Where this is not possible, they have the right to just and fair compensation. Unless otherwise freely agreed upon by the peoples concerned, compensation shall take the form of lands, territories and resources equal in quality, size and legal status.

Article 28

Indigenous peoples have the right to the conservation, restoration and protection of the total environment and the productive capacity of their lands, territories and resources, as well as to assistance for this purpose from States and through international cooperation. Military activities shall not take place in the lands and territories of indigenous peoples, unless otherwise freely agreed upon by the peoples concerned.

States shall take effective measures to ensure that no storage or disposal of hazardous materials shall take place in the lands and territories of indigenous peoples.

States shall also take effective measures to ensure, as needed, that programmes for monitoring, maintaining and restoring the health of indigenous peoples, as developed and implemented by the peoples affected by such materials, are duly implemented.

Article 29

Indigenous peoples are entitled to the recognition of the full ownership, control and protection of their cultural and intellectual property.

They have the right to special measures to control, develop and protect their sciences, technologies and cultural manifestations, including human and other genetic resources, seeds, medicines, knowledge of the properties of fauna and flora, oral traditions, literatures, designs and visual and performing arts.

Article 30

Indigenous peoples have the right to determine and develop priorities and strategies for the development or use of their lands, territories and other resources, including the right to require that States obtain their free and informed consent prior to the approval of any project affecting their lands, territories and other resources, particularly in connection with the development, utilization or exploitation of mineral, water or other resources. Pursuant to agreement with the indigenous peoples concerned, just and fair compensation shall be provided for any such activities and measures taken to mitigate adverse environmental, economic, social, cultural or spiritual impact.

PART VII

Article 31

Indigenous peoples, as a specific form of exercising their right to self-determination, have the right to autonomy or self-government in matters relating to their internal and local affairs, including culture, religion, education, information, media, health, housing, employment, social welfare, economic activities, land and resources management, environment and entry by non-members, as well as ways and means for financing these autonomous functions.

Article 32

Indigenous peoples have the collective right to determine their own citizenship in accordance with their customs and traditions. Indigenous citizenship does not impair the right of indigenous individuals to obtain citizenship of the States in which they live.

Indigenous peoples have the right to determine the structures and to select the membership of their institutions in accordance with their own procedures.

Article 33

Indigenous peoples have the right to promote, develop and maintain their institutional structures and their distinctive juridical customs, traditions, procedures and practices, in accordance with internationally recognized human rights standards.

Article 34

Indigenous peoples have the collective right to determine the responsibilities of individuals to their communities.

Article 35

Indigenous peoples, in particular those divided by international borders, have the right to maintain and develop contacts, relations and cooperation, including activities for spiritual, cultural, political, economic and social purposes, with other peoples across borders.

States shall take effective measures to ensure the exercise and implementation of this right.

Article 36

Indigenous peoples have the right to the recognition, observance and enforcement of treaties, agreements and other constructive arrangements concluded with States or their successors, according to their original spirit and intent, and to have States honor and respect such treaties, agreements and other constructive arrangements. Conflicts and disputes which cannot otherwise be settled should be submitted to competent international bodies agreed to by all parties concerned.

PART VIII

Article 37

States shall take effective and appropriate measures, in consultation with the indigenous peoples concerned, to give full effect to the provisions of this Declaration. The rights recognized herein shall be adopted and included in national legislation in such a manner that indigenous peoples can avail themselves of such rights in practice.

Article 38

Indigenous peoples have the right to have access to adequate financial and technical assistance, from States and through international cooperation, to pursue freely their political, economic, social, cultural and spiritual development and for the enjoyment of the rights and freedoms recognized in this Declaration.

Article 39

Indigenous peoples have the right to have access to and prompt decision through mutually acceptable and fair procedures for the resolution of conflicts and disputes with States, as well as to effective remedies for all infringements of their individual and collective rights. Such a decision shall take into consideration the customs, traditions, rules and legal systems of the indigenous peoples concerned.

Article 40

The organs and specialized agencies of the United Nations system and other intergovernmental organizations shall contribute to the full realization of the provisions of this Declaration through the mobilization, *inter alia*, of financial cooperation and technical assistance. Ways and means of ensuring participation of indigenous peoples on issues affecting them shall be established.

Article 41

The United Nations shall take the necessary steps to ensure the implementation of this Declaration including the creation of a body at the highest level with special competence in this field and with the direct participation of indigenous peoples. All United Nations bodies shall promote respect for and full application of the provisions of this Declaration.

PART IX

Article 42

The rights recognized herein constitute the minimum standards for the survival, dignity and well-being of the indigenous peoples of the world.

Article 43

All the rights and freedoms recognized herein are equally guaranteed to male and female indigenous individuals.

Article 44

Nothing in this Declaration may be construed as diminishing or extinguishing existing or future rights indigenous peoples may have or acquire.

Article 45

Nothing in this Declaration may be interpreted as implying for any State, group or person any right to engage in any activity or to perform any act contrary to the Charter of the United Nations.

PHOTOGRAPHIC CREDITS

INFORMATION SOURCES

Those who wish additional information on the self-determination and sovereignty of indigenous peoples or who wish to lend financial support may do so by contacting the following organizations:

The Native American Council of New York City
404 Lafayette St.
New York, NY 10003

Solidarity Foundation
310 West 52nd St.
New York, NY 10019